Defying the Trend

Business Ethics and Corporate Morality
from a Faith Perspective

Defying the Trend

*Business Ethics and Corporate Morality
from a Faith Perspective*

by Jeffrey P. Wincel

God's Embrace Publishing
728 E. 8th St. #3
Holland, MI 49423

International Standard Book Number- 9780557328352 (paperback)

Printed and bound by Lulu Publishing

Library of Congress Control Number: 2010902603

I dedicate this book to my wife Heather, and my kids Emily, Matthew, Alison, JP, Matt, and Ryan.

All my love…..jpw

Contents

Introduction

Commentary about ethics seems at first glance to be a simple and straight forward discussion about "appropriate" behavior. The practical among us would say that it is simply about knowing the right thing to do and doing it. Academics and theologians however would say that it is not that simple; they would argue that there needs to be a great deal of specificity regarding the meaning of "ethics" and "morality." They would want to see a method to distinguish between different ethical approaches. "Natural law" must be differentiated from culturally grounded deontology[1], or to a social-contract ethics. Care would be needed as to not confuse assertions of "situational ethics" to utilitarianism. They would see a greater complexity and sophistication of these various ethical models than the average person gives them credit for, or perhaps even cares to understand.

Many of the complex situations in life seemingly don't fall so easily into a religiously-based natural law approach. For example, how would this engage some complex and morally ambiguous situations where the issues you face may be more so in the realm of legality rather than morality – e.g., insider-trading. Issues such as executive compensation, are not legal issues (at least, were not until recent events in Congress) but ethical issues. To the "practical" observer, there would be clear cut answer to these issues, while

---

[1] Deontology is essentially a type of ethics which judges the morality of an action based on its adherence to a rule or rules. This is contrasted to "virtue ethics" which is based upon personal morality, or consequentialism which emphasizes the consequences of ethical decisions. See: http://plato.stanford.edu/entries/ethics-virtue/ (accessed 1/17/10)

mic/theologian would see a deontological approach with one
ilitarianism another, and social-contract yet another.

Simply said, this book examines the effects and affects of ethics and morality on the *success or failure* of business. More than that, this book is about honor. It is about integrity. It is about noble behavior of one's self, of one's company, and towards one's world. This book is about recognizing that our role in this world, regardless of professional or religious views, is to be in the service of others. Through that service not only do we achieve the business success we are seeking, but we also strengthen the personal bonds we have with each other. These ideas aren't some utopian hope of the future, but a reflection of the realities of cultural growth; and perhaps even about cultural survival. Every culture around the world possesses the expectation of moral behavior of its society. With the impact of the expanding global economy, this expectation is now demanded of every business everywhere in the world. As a result, this book also examines the impact of religious and natural law on business behavior, and how they are integrated into global corporate action.

The changing nature of global competition and social expectations has caused businesses to find themselves in increasingly challenging ethical dilemmas. There have been many highly publicized failures of moral integrity that have destroyed companies, destroyed individuals, and destroyed communities. "Appropriate" business behavior can only take place when executives recognize that it is the needs and demands of *all* of its constituents which determine the company's strategic and operational objectives. These actions really are the basis for ethical behavior.

> *More than that, this book is about honor. It is about integrity.*

The Integrity Gap

When the topic of morality is called into question, many businesses simply do not know how to deal with the topic. Author John Maxwell writes about a national sales meeting where one of the senior vice presidents proposes a discussion on ethics as part of the objectives and strategies that are being laid out for the coming year. With the proposal, the room falls silent. No one knows what to do or say. Finally, the CEO of the company tables the topic, later explaining his belief that the meeting is supposed to be motivating and that ethics is "such a negative subject".[2]

Our best business academic institutions also appear to fall short in failing to include ethics as part of their core curriculum.[3] Maxwell writes about a University of Michigan course description for a class titled "The Ethics of Corporate Management". Amazingly, the course description specifically excludes an evaluation of personal ethics, stating "This course is not concerned with the personal moral issues of honesty and truthfulness." So exactly how are ethics discussed in this class where honesty and truthfulness are not important? Likewise, among its standard academic offerings, the college text book publisher McGraw-Hill Irwin describes the in-class use of one of its books using "one's own personal ethical basis to understand case discussions in ethical problems."[4] This statement can be viewed by many as an alarming

---

[2] John C. Maxwell, *There's No Such Thing as "Business" Ethics: There's Only One Rule For Making Decisions*, Warner Faith, (August 2003), pg 6.

[3] Most colleges and universities include courses on all types of ethics, but few require more than introductory ethics courses for its business students.

[4] Laura P. Hartman, DePaul University Perspectives in Business Ethics with PowerWeb, 2nd Edition, McGraw-Hill Irwin. This is not a criticism of Laura Hartman, as her work seems to be focused on virtue ethics – that is, an emphasis on acting morally out of who one is at one's core. She appears to create a distinction in that virtue ethics is not the same as relativism, and in fact is closer to a religious based ethics than many other theories. The title of her most recent

example of relativism and political correctness. Can a student who believes that "anything goes", pass the class on ethics regardless of how "unethical" their ethics may be? Despite curriculum including courses on ethics, and while claiming academic freedom for its professors in the material they teach, most of our major universities seem to be reluctant to tackle the tough subject of trying to define the basis of ethics outside of secular philosophy and their application in all areas of life. There is a seemingly endless stream of apologetics in the way in which ethics and morality are spoken of.

> *The workplace often provides an environment in which everyday beliefs and behaviors can be put aside without regret.*

These stories represent the "Integrity Gap" which exists in many people. The workplace often provides an environment in which everyday beliefs and behaviors can be put aside without regret. Companies foster the belief that the rules which apply at work are different than those which apply outside the office. The courage to step out on a limb (from an ethical viewpoint) is a courage that seldom exists. The consequences of doing so can mean an end to a career; it can mean an end to company respect. It can ultimately mean career isolation or being ostracized.

Work organizations survive on the concept of tribal thought, and any movement away from that tribal thought becomes frightening. It is shunned by the rest of the tribe. In this way, only the tribal (business)

---

textbook (2008) bears this out better: *Business Ethics: Decision-Making for Personal Integrity and Social Responsibility.*

leaders, whether formal or informal, can lead the company back toward ethical behavior. However, it is the personal acts of ethical behavior that cause the leaders to stand up and take notice of the shift that needs to happen – astute leaders recognize when the groundswell of a movement is taking place.

Perhaps the main ethical approach I'm writing about is virtue ethics. Virtue ethics is grounded in Aristotle and informs much of Christian ethical thinking. Virtue ethics is an ethical commitment by each individual and is grounded in who they choose to *be* as persons. In this, professional, social and religious affiliation will play a large role in defining the ethical commitments made by individuals.

Ethical-Theological Approach

It was clear to me that there is a tremendous gap in our world where anyone is willing to bridge the divide between the two worlds of business and ethics. Nearly everyone I spoke to or interviewed was worried about how they would be perceived by others if they "really" talked about how they feel. In researching other books, there were either books on business with "secular ethics" or religious books; there was nearly nothing with both. Even the publishers were "afraid" to touch the realm of others. The business publishers considered this a religious/spiritual book, while the spiritual publishers considered this a business book. None wanted to cross the bridge and link the two.

A number of years ago, I began to dedicate a portion of the professional presentations I made, or every seminar I led to the topic of ethical business behavior. At first I was fearful that this would be perceived as "weak" and not only distract from the business material I was presenting, but also backfire on the ethical message as well. I couldn't have been more wrong! After every event, I am now surrounded by throngs of people thirsting to talk more about the ethical challenges they face, and how they can meet these challenges. There are now times when the entire presentation is based on the ethical issues, with the business backdrop as the context for how these play out.

> *After every event, I am now surrounded by throngs of people thirsting to talk more about the ethical challenges they face, and how they can meet these challenges.*

Since morality (behavior) and ethics (ideology) fall into three broad schools of thought, namely, ethical theism, ethical humanism, and ethical naturalism, it is important (as I learned from Dr. Ascough) to identify with clarity from which school of thought we have drawn our discussion. For example, writing from an ethical theist's perspective, one must identify the theistic basis they are drawing from, e.g., Catholic, Protestant, Jewish, Islamic, etc. For this book, I am writing largely from a Christian perspective, especially from a Catholic Social viewpoint. Realizing this, it is then equally important to indentify from within which school of thought we are operating. In other words, the theological context of our discussion of business ethics must be established.

The theological context from which my view of ethics and morality stems is an ethical theism based on an Augustinian personalist perspective that can be linked in modern thought with experiential (existential) philosophy as described by Karl Barth, Christian Phenomenology as used by Pope John Paul II, and the ressourcement theology of Henri de Lubac, Hans Urs von Balthasar, Joseph Cardinal Ratzinger (Pope Benedict XVI), and others. In the context of this book, the emphasis of this perspective is a return to the theologically and philosophically based behaviors as understood by the early Church Fathers, reflected in private devotion, and demonstrated in public life. This perspective harmonizes with the efforts of the Vatican Council II which, in part, sought greater participation of the believer in the life of the church and in the world. The personalist context of ethics and morality described here seeks a greater degree of participation of these theologies and philosophies in the life of the business, especially in the work place.

This view of ethics contrasts that of a Thomistic perspective which proposes that by rationalistic codification, behavior can be prescribed through a given set of scholastic arguments. Contemporary theology sees this played out in neo-scholastic movements. Augustinian personalism has been said to be a "viable alternative to the prevailing impersonalism in Western culture,"[5] an impersonalism which neo-scholastic Thomistic theology can become. The "roots" (epistemology and ontology) of Augustinian personalism are coupled (integrated) in such a way that there exists virtually no distinction, such as developed in the scholastic and neo-scholastic traditions, between philosophy and theology – the essence of who we are in God is inseparable from our place and interaction in the world.

> *What is taken as obvious by Augustine – particularly our personal and immediate participation in God – seems axiomatically absurd to the normal operational assumptions of our cultural life form.*

Saints were always the leading theologians and vice versa in this tradition. Evagrius Pontius (346 – c.399) wrote in the 4th century, "He who prays truly is a theologian, and he is a theologian only who prays truly." The modern split between theology and spirituality, much less between theology and philosophy, seems incomprehensible to

---

[5] Paul Tyson, *Western Culture and the 'Hypothesis of God,"* <u>Appraisal</u> Vol. 5 No. 4, October 2005

theologians steeped in the Augustinian tradition. To this point Paul Tyson writes "what is taken as obvious by Augustine – particularly our personal and immediate participation in God – seems axiomatically absurd to the normal operational assumptions of our cultural life form." It is exactly this argument and reality that I attempt to counteract. Our personal and immediate participation in God is what necessitates a higher level of corporate behavior.

The personalist perspective is most clearly reflected in Chapter 8 – An Anatomy of a Company, where human traits are given to a company and its culture. The purpose of this "humanization" is to demonstrate the inextricable link between the nature of "participation in the Divine" and our participation in the profane. Humanity *should not* separate itself from its fundamental values of fairness and equity, but also *can not* separate the individual person from their personal participation and experience of the Divine.

While I address the uncomfortable issues of personal behavior; talk openly about the impact of religion and God on society and business; and speak of personal honor and integrity, I make no apologies for any of it. Neither do I seek to purposely offend the reader. This book will make some readers uncomfortable. It if does, then perhaps it has accomplished its task. This book will make some readers angry. If it does, then perhaps it has accomplished its task. This book will be seen by some readers as naïve. If it does, then perhaps it has accomplished its task. Its objective isn't conversion to a theistic view of business, but to encourage thought of the possibility of what faith could bring to the business place. What I hope to accomplish is to help the readers to recognize that ultimately our job as business leaders is to understand rather than be understood; is to hear rather than be heard; and is to serve rather than be served.

Acknowledgements

Every book and creative work is never a solitary effort. They are products of inspiration and collaboration of many wonderful people. For the creative and dynamic spirit they've brought to this book, I first would like to thank the visionary business, academic, and spiritual leaders who so graciously volunteered their time and ideas to the interviews which end each chapter. Dr. Richard Ascough, Professor of Theology, Queens College Toronto provided me especially important critical review, insuring that I treat the serious subject of ethics and morality with more than just a superficial gloss. Without these advisors, the book would only be the ramblings of some guy with an idea; with them, the book is a reflection of the realities of the ethical world – of what is and what could be.

Next, I have to give my greatest thanks to my friend and colleague Hazel Beck. As collaborators in the dog-eat-dog business world, we have together experience the good, bad, and ugly of what the world has to offer. Hazel was my unofficial editor of many versions of the manuscript for this book and her suggestions were invaluable.

Finally, I thank my fellow Aspirants/Candidates and those who continually help me on my never ending journey to find the true nature and spirit of God.

Chapter One – Ethics, Law, Freedom, & God

Introduction

I began work on this book in 2005 following the debacles of Enron, Tyco, MCI, Arthur Anderson, and others. Never would I have thought that another ethical crisis would eclipse this failure of corporate behavior. Then came the housing crisis, the banking crisis, and the near fatal collapse of the economy in 2008 and 2009. Each time, the failure of business leaders, companies, and governmental agencies achieved a new low. It became clear to me that despite the publishers' reluctance to offer a new book on ethics, our culture has found itself on the precipice of great travail. Not only is another book on ethics and morality necessary, but many are and are critical for the survival of our economy and society. Critical in that it points the way back toward a culture that transcends its own greedy motives, and returns us to society based upon our national principles of providing for the common good.[6]

When we talk of business ethics and corporate morality, we are talking about both the behavior (morality) and the ideology (ethics) of what it means to serve as leaders and stewards in our places of business and commerce. Ethics and morality are strong words and strong concepts loaded with expectation, misunderstanding and even dread.

---

[6] A strong case can be made that from the founding of our nation, the ideal of providing for the common good was never one held by businesses. Businesses and business owners have exploited employees for their own benefit with the common good only as necessary to insure their survival.

They are also ideas that we seemingly see very little of in our everyday business world. While the litany of high profile business "events" seems to result in more discussion about these topics, there is little evidence of them in practice. While the discussion of morality and ethics is growing today because of the immediate impact that corporate scandals are now having on our lives, in many ways ironically, our reaction to these corporate scandals frequently results in a behavior almost like the grim curiosity shown when passing a tragic car accident.

Sadly, although we are talking more about the behavior, our reaction is usually to either take delight in the plight of others, or clucking about how they should have known better. Seldom do we see evidence of how to *learn* from the trials of others. Throughout this book I will highlight examples of both sides of the ethical coin to shed light on the possibility of learning from the mistakes of others; to help our own business, and even those of others; to avoid morally questionable behavior; and to recognize that success is based on business leaders' ability to serve others.

Why are we ethically challenged?

With all the recent events culminating in the greatest recession in our lifetime, it seems that ethics in business is almost as foreign as ethics in American government. Somewhere along the way, there developed the idea that behavior in business could follow the "all is fair in love and war" mentality. The individual and company behaviors that you see everyday in business are often in stark contrast to the personal ethics and behavior business leaders show everywhere else in life. The ideas of "moral corporate action" and "ethical professional behavior" are fundamental ideas that are at once simple to embrace, but often difficult to practice. When we see all the recent corporate scandals, read headlines about executive prosecution and hear about endless corporate abuses, we may wonder whatever happened to corporate morality.

> *It seem like ethics in business is almost as foreign as ethics in American government. Somewhere along the way, there developed the idea that behavior in business could follow the "all is fair in love and war" mentality.*

John Maxwell, in his book, *There's no Such Thing as Business Ethics,*[7] writes that there are no separate ethics or ways to behave simply because you are at work. He says that there is only one set of ethics for everything in life. Based on his thought, I ask, "Can we *really* have *any* ethics if we are able to behave unethically or immorally at work?" Or, do we simply accept the lack of ethics by justifying it as "just the way it is"? I know that I am not alone when I can think of many men and women (some of them even close friends) who are "like someone else" when we see how they behave at work versus at home. Are we one of those people?

Companies, and the executives who run them, generally do not ignore complying with the law or seek to operate in an unethical fashion. In fact, most business enterprises (especially the largest) seek to follow the <u>letter</u> of the law – and may even have a staff of attorneys on hand to ensure compliance. The unfortunate reality is that following only the letter of the law (and more likely finding "legal" ways to bend the law) does not reflect the spirit or even underlying moral basis of the law. It is the absence of the underlying moral foundations that results in questionable behavior. More often than not, the single imperative in business is profit - without consideration of how that profit is achieved. However, profit alone does not create the ethically devoid environment where anything goes. It is the single-minded pursuit of profit and lack of

---

[7] John C. Maxwell, *There's No Such Thing as "Business" Ethics: There's Only One Rule For Making Decisions*, Warner Faith, (August 2003).

ethical leadership that creates the conditions in which morally questionable actions occur. It's like the adage that it is "the *love* of money that is the root of all evil", not the money itself.

> **It is the single-minded pursuit of profit and lack of ethical leadership that creates the conditions in which morally questionable actions occur.**

Society's influence on behavior

It's almost impossible to try to define our modern acceptance of business behavior. The reality show "The Apprentice", a show in which would be future executives try to outperform and out maneuver each other for the chance to work for Donald Trump is an example of the prevalent ambiguity of moral centeredness in business. A key feature of the show is the betrayal and backstabbing between contestants to be sure they are not the one "fired". Is this show just TV or does it reflect our modern society? Either way, it now is sending a message that there are "special" behaviors that are required to be successful.

Understanding the basis of business morality cannot exist without an examination of the effects of modernity on business, cultural and religious society. The interplay of these three basic foundations of our society sometimes coexists in an uneasy way. We see this every day when we are told that we shouldn't talk about religion or politics or we risk offending others around us. We are supposed to talk about "safe" things – like business!

Our 21st century actions and beliefs within the United States are almost solely based on the history of social and religious changes in the 20th century.[8] The early 20th century was a time in which we saw

---

[8] Prior to the 20th century, the agrarian society in which Americans lived was one often marked by illiteracy, with ethical behavior dictated by strict cultural restrictions on speech, freedom and

substantial and largely uncontrolled abuses in the areas of business, culture, and religion, but also a period that created unparalleled growth in cultural and human expansion. The mid 20th century was generally a time of the growth of curiosity, freedom and self-expression and perhaps the beginning of spiritual renewal. Finally, the late 20th century through today seems to be characterized by the divorce of religion from all other forms of societal intercourse. While religious and spiritual renewal seems to have grown in personal ways in the latter half of the century, it was also consciously removed from our public lives – often with venom and violence.

The funny thing is that this removal of God and morality really is unique to the U.S. In nearly every social and religious tradition, there is an accepted belief that the society functions much more smoothly if it possess and exhibits a belief in ethical behavior.[9] While we, as a Judeo-Christian society, say that not only do we share the belief of ethical behavior but champion it around the world, we often find ourselves without credibility. This lack of credibility is due to our "not walking the talk" of what we claim to believe. We "pontificate" about how the rest of the world should behave without actually following it ourselves.

> *While religious and spiritual renewal seems to have grown in personal ways in the latter half of the century, it was also consciously removed from our public lives – often with venom and violence.*

---

where expression was institutionally curtailed. With the rapid advancement in industrialization and resulting urbanization, ethical certainties became less clear and behavior easier to obscure.

[9] Admittedly, other "Christian" countries, especially in Western Europe, have a far less overt expression of Christianity in their daily lives. This is contrasted in Eastern Europe and Latin America where expression of faith are found throughout the culture, including the workplace.

Global Morality – Natural Law

Many of our moral beliefs are actually shared around the world. This culturally shared sense of ethical good comes from the idea that a common natural law exists and is relevant to all cultures and in all times. Natural law has been the topic for social and theological contemplation for thousands of years, ranging from being accepted as fact throughout the culture (world) to being questioned as true and relevant by many.

Today, there are scholars who debate the idea of cultural or situational ethics, suggesting that ethics are based only on the specific culture in which they are applied and specific to the circumstance of those living with them. While we certainly see what appears to be evidence of situational ethics, this "evidence" doesn't make the existence of situational ethics (or lack of natural law) true. The idea of "where there is smoke there must be fire" has often led us down the wrong path. I accept the idea of natural law as an underlying basis for good in humanity. I share the view of the theologian Thomas Aquinas who held at the heart of his beliefs that humanity is compelled by nature to pursue good and avoid evil.[10] The preamble to our Declaration of Independence recognizes both natural law and the source of that natural law when it says, "to assume among the powers of the earth, the separate and equal station to which the laws of nature and of nature's God entitle them."

A prevalent type of situational ethics is a version called utilitarianism. This type of ethical doctrine suggests that the criteria which drive or is the virtue of action are those that provide the greatest

---

[10] *Treatise on the Law*, St. Thomas Aquinas, Summa Theologiae, *I-II*; qq. 90-97, ChIII, ss5, [277]

happiness to the greatest number of people. With this the value of any action is based upon its "usefulness". The University of San Diego, an independent Catholic University, addresses ethical utilitarianism as part of its curriculum and Ethics Matters series. Dr. Lawrence Hinman writes that among the basic insights of utilitarianism is that "the purpose of morality is to make the world a better place", "morality is about producing good consequences, not having good intentions", and "we should do whatever will bring the most benefit (i.e., intrinsic value) to all of humanity."[11] Dr. Hinman does not suggest that he holds this view; simply that it is the common view of utilitarianism. The danger of this type of ethical belief is that the ideal of the "greater good" can be very attractive despite the fact that utilitarianism emphasizes consequences, not intentions. We frequently identify this view with the perspective of the ends justifying the means. The means by which the ends are accomplished can easily deteriorate into *any* means, even if those means are considered immoral. Ironically, utilitarianism is a morally demanding view requiring personal interests and desires being set aside in order to maximize the outcome (utility).

Ethics & morality pays!

I don't know how many times I've heard businessmen and businesswomen say that the idea of business ethics is "quaint", but in the real "dog-eat-dog" world anything goes to ensure survival. There is truly a belief that without this behavior (dog-eat-dog aggressiveness); a company simply cannot be profitable or successful. The thing is - all the data point to the opposite as being true. Not only are "ethically" based

---

[11] *Fundamental Tenets of Utilitarianism*, Dr. Lawrence M. Hinman, PhD., pg 4., http://ethics.sandiego.edu/presentations/Theory/Utilitarianism/index.asp, accessed 7/8/09.

companies more profitable, they are also better places to work and have higher customer satisfaction.

In 2003, a leading business magazine featured an article which developed a profile of the type of company that exhibited the highest level of ethical and moral behavior. According to the article, family-owned companies with outside boards of directors were those who achieved this distinction. The primary reason is that as a family owned company there was no distinction between business performance and personal performance. Behavior at work directly reflected the employee's personal integrity. The presence of an outside board of directors helps keep a "neutral" perspective so that the family members avoid turning excessively inward. Sometimes morality needs a little help.

But it's not just family-owned businesses and companies that can be successful. One study examining the profit returns of "traditional" versus "ethically-based" companies found that traditional companies were outperformed financially by 96% per year over a 30-year period. The study showed that $30k invested in the Dow composite 30 years ago would have been worth $134k or 447% return (14.89%/yr) versus the same amount invested in a socially and ethically responsible portfolio, which would be worth $1 million or 3,333.33% return (111.11%/year).[12]

To have ethics or not?

In the highly competitive business of discount retail, there are two giants that are often reported on. The first of these is Wal-Mart. When Sam Walton was alive, the business practices employed by Wal-Mart

---

[12] Executive Leadership Foundation, *Absolute Ethics*, pg. 24

were seldom questioned with respect to their acceptability. In fact, Wal-Mart was often held up as an example of ethics, especially related to its involvement in the communities it served. That has seemed to change with Sam Walton's death.

In the business magazine Fast Company, the December 2003 cover story was titled "The Wal-Mart You Don't Know"[13] which detailed the ethically questionable behavior of Wal-Mart's treatment towards it suppliers. The article presents a pretty ugly story for what a company considers necessary to make money. In order to achieve its #1 position as a retailer, and achieve its low-cost guarantee, the article alleges that Wal-Mart will either blackball or even force suppliers into bankruptcy if they do not comply with Wal-Mart's pricing and sourcing rules. Wal-Mart also struggles in its relationship with its employees regarding treatment, work conditions, wages and benefits.[14]

Compare that to the other discount giant Costco. The business model is entirely different at Costco. The company's strategy is to maintain low prices by limiting itself to a standard fixed mark-up compared to Wal-Mart's aggressive supplier tactics. With this approach, Costco is significantly out performing Wal-Mart's Sam's Club chain. Figures detailed in Fortune Magazine demonstrate this:[15]

> "Sam's Club has 71% more U.S. stores than Costco (532 to 312), yet for the year ended Aug. 31, Costco had 5% more sales ($34.4 billion vs. an estimated $32.9 billion). The average Costco store

---

[13] Charles Fishman, *The Wal-Mart You Don't Know*, Fast Company Magazine, Dec. 2003, Issue 77, pg. 68. See also: http://www.fastcompany.com/magazine/77/walmart.html

[14] New York Times, *In-House Audit Says Wal-Mart Violated Labor Laws*, January 13, 2004, by Steve Green House.
http://query.nytimes.com/gst/abstract.html?res=F30714FF39540C708DDDA80894DC404482

[15] http://www.fortune.com/fortune/investing/articles/0%2C15114%2C538834%2C00.html

generates nearly double the revenue of a Sam's Club ($112 million vs. $63 million)".

The basis for moral action

In our nature to pursue good ethical behavior we must believe, like Maxwell, that ethics apply to all areas of our lives. Behavior in business is (or should be) ultimately defined by the capacity of service to the various business constituents. Service to others lies at the heart of the concepts of natural law. This service is made even clearer when we examine the idea of the influence of religious beliefs on our business behavior. Ethics are not situational, but based on the acceptance of religious morality. Clearly (or maybe not so clearly), I'm mixing a number of ethical and moral views here where service points to a social contract/social rights approach. Where as a strict interpretation of natural law would follow a rigorous deontological view where rules are followed no matter what, because they came from God; the nuanced service view suggests that within natural law there is a personalist experience of God. That experience is translated into service and care for others – it is the application of the "golden rule" that cuts across many religious traditions.

Although we may choose not to acknowledge a religious moral basis because of the discomfort it may bring, the basic elements which should drive business ethics and corporate morality are natural law and revealed law. This acceptance doesn't mean that there is only one religious tradition that has to be followed, but as the creator and propagator of natural and revealed law, God must be at the root of ethical corporate behavior.

> *The basic elements which must drive business ethics and corporate morality are natural law and revealed law*

Christian tradition and teaching has consistently taught that natural law is the fundamental basis for morality and ethical behavior. Pope John Paul II wrote of social justice and ethics in the context of the treatment of workers to the modern generation in the encyclical *Veritatis Splendor.* At the root of his ethical argument is that ethics come from God through natural law. He writes: that a basic morality is unbounded by time and space, existing in the world regardless of person, place, or time.[16] He writes that morality is not dependent on our ascent, as the basis of morality comes from the natural laws of God (whether you believe in God or not).[17] John Paul adds that in unselfish surrender, humanity is free to derive grace from this morality.[18] Paradoxically, one can say that from these three points one can extract moral action as an obligation arising out of honoring the laws by *freely* choosing to obey them.

As we look at how business ethics and corporate morality are framed in every culture by the ideas of natural law and a divine guidance, we have to consider how these things take form in the everyday world. Who is responsible? How do we act? What is the purpose of ethics? As I said previously, behavior in business is ultimately defined by the capacity of service to the various business constituents. The responsibility of exhibiting the ethical behavior falls not only on the leaders of a company, but to all employees, managers, executives and owners in equal fashion. It is the examination of how each of these "constituents" is personally responsible for ethical behavior to the others that will be the focus of this book.

---

[16] *Veritatis Splendor* (The Splendor of Truth), Pauline Press, Vatican Translation, 1:6-7 (pg 16-17)
[17] *Veritatis Splendor,* 1:42-43 (pg 58-59)

[18] *Veritatis Splendor,* 1:8-9 (pg 17-19); 1:11 (pg. 21)

> *As we look at how business ethics and corporate morality are framed in every culture ... we have to consider how these things take form in the everyday world.*

Questions to Consider

1) Do I understand what ethics and morality mean?
2) Do I apply these ethical standards equally in all areas of my life?
3) How often do I justify my behavior based on the situation or action of others?
4) What is at the root of my ethics? Is it my own standards or those set by God?
5) How can I make my ethics evident in my daily behavior?

Chapter Two – The Constituents

The Ingredients to Business

To fully understand the factors contributing to the effects of corporate moral action, you need to understand the "constituents" that are served by all companies. But, what exactly are constituents? In the simplest sense, a constituent is anyone that is required to create and sustain something – like a business. Constituents are the ingredients necessary to make something work. In business, you need *customers* to sell things to; you need *owners* to provide capital (cash) to buy the stuff to make things with and build them in; you need *employees* to actually make the things (products or services); you need *suppliers* to provide the stuff to make things with; and you need a *community* in which to exist. If any one of these parts ceases to exist or performs poorly, the company suffers and itself may cease to exist.

> *Too often, the best intentions are left on the conference room floor.*

How you behave toward these constituents directly determines the *quality* of business ethics and corporate morality. For something like ethics and morality to have any real meaning, there has to be a *conscious* effort to understand the appropriate behavior and expectations of the constituents or "stakeholders". Ethical businesses develop business plans and corporate strategies that serve to satisfy these requirements, but it takes a real effort to actually put them in place.

Perception is reality

In their book, *Credibility: How Leaders Gain and Lose It, Why People Demand It*, Barry Pozner and James Kouzes make a simple point: "DWYSYWD" – Do what you said you would do.[19] Too often, the best intentions are left on the conference room floor. While the executive management may talk about the appropriate ways to behave or how to meet the needs of its constituents, all this seems to be forgotten when it comes to "real" corporate life. But it's not only the executives, it's the account managers, it's the purchasing managers, it's the HR managers; it's all of us. Simply living up to our commitments and doing what we said we would do is the easiest way to build a moral and ethical foundation.

I once worked for an executive who in a former life was a general manager of an automotive assembly plant. He would tell a story where the same circumstances within the plant would have two very different interpretations. He would meet with his management team where he would be told how well things were going, both internally and with customers. He would then walk out into the plant and be told how horribly things were going. It didn't take him long to realize that the truth lay probably somewhere in the middle and that the guys telling him how good or how bad things were represented the two vocal fringes. It was clear that reality was very different from the 2 sets of perception.

Nearly everyone who has worked in the corporate world has experienced the "all employee meeting". This meeting is one where the

---

[19] Barry Pozner and James Kouzes, *Credibility: How Leaders Gain and Lose It, Why People Demand It*, January 2003, Wiley, John & Sons, Incorporated.

company management brings the employees together to tell them about the "bright future" or the "changes to come" or "the end of downsizing", etc. When the meeting is finished, a few employees comment to the management team that they appreciate the information and welcome whatever is coming. The management team goes away with a sense that they've made the connection to the employees and knows that the sun will shine through! Most of the employees leave the meeting thinking, "what a bunch of $%!#" or some other colorful adjective. They generally think that this is just another in a series of changes, promises, whatever, and that "they (the management) just don't get it". For both, the perception has become the reality – regardless of what the reality is. Also, in both cases, neither is serving or satisfying its constituents very well. This meeting could easily be one with a customer or with suppliers and the outcome would be the same.

> *While those shaping the culture of the company may believe that they are providing the leadership towards ethical behavior, the employee perception of their performance may be completely different.*

One last story: I recently had the opportunity to hear Dr. John Maxwell speak at a key note address in front of an audience of over 5,000. Dr. Maxwell is a renowned author and scholar on leadership, business, ethics, religion, and more. It was obvious from his presentation and from his books that he takes seriously the idea of valuing people, striving to be ethical in his endeavors, and treating each person with the "golden rule" – treat others the way you want to be treated. After the presentation, Dr. Maxwell was heading out to fly home to spend time with his wife, children, and grandchildren. As he was making his way to the car to get to the airport, a number of people stopped him to ask him to sign some of his books, to ask his opinion on some aspect of his presentation, or even to explore business opportunities. Because of his tight schedule, Dr. Maxwell wasn't able to provide much time or attention to these requests. I had a person comment to me that they couldn't believe that he was being so rude. Obviously, their perception of what he had said on stage didn't match what they were seeing. He was not doing "what he said he would do". After some discussion and persuasion, I was able to convince this person that because of Dr. Maxwell's success, I was certain that there were tremendous demands on his time and talent, and that, coupled with the tight schedule, simply resulted in what we were seeing. There is no doubt that a man like Dr. Maxwell has the highest level of ethics and integrity, but perceptions can create a different reality. Ultimately, it's these "one-by-one" reactions that can influence an entire company or culture.

These stories simply represent what will ultimately be the reaction to a company's behavior toward moral and ethical issues and its service to its constituents. While those shaping the culture of the company may believe that they are providing the leadership (not simply the management) towards ethical behavior, the perception of their performance may be completely different. Individual and group perceptions reflect the effectiveness of the service to constituents – from the ideas to reality.

Moral & Religious foundation of service

The idea of service to business constituents is best articulated by the theories and practices developed by Joe Scanlon in the 1950s. His ideas were based on the ideas of equity and participation. (Chapter 3 will detail Scanlon's beliefs regarding employee participation). Scanlon believed that an organization could only excel if it tapped into the creative nature of its employees through decision making participation, and directly rewarded the employees for the results. He was able to create the idea of employees as constituents to be served, while being able to also serve the owner constituents. While Scanlon advocates don't generally speak of the religious foundation of their actions, many of the leading practitioners also possess a clear religious commitment that is reflected in their businesses.

While it's less than popular in today's culture to say so, I firmly believe that the foundation of service to business constituents cannot be separated from religious belief. Ethics and morality are inseparably based on a consistent set of beliefs that can transcend generations and cultures. Without a fundamental stability or "north star" to provide reference, ethics and morality have no meaning. To have a lasting and permanent effect in business, business ethics and corporate morality must be based on the religious ideals of natural and revealed law. Natural law is that internal feeling or knowledge of what is good or bad. What does your gut instinct tell you? More often than not, business leaders either ignore or learn to silence the "inner voice" – their Jiminy Cricket! Revealed laws are the laws we learned about every week as a child in Sunday school – such as: don't lie, don't cheat and don't steal. Our religious traditions provide these guidelines for the service to all constituents – business leaders simply have to know and follow these.

> *Without a fundamental stability or "north star" to provide reference, ethics and morality have no meaning.*

While the natural and revealed laws themselves provide an outstanding framework that any business (or really any activity in life) would benefit in following, the moral basis for these laws stems from God. As the creator and propagator of natural and revealed law, God must also be at the root of ethical corporate behavior. The responsibility for exhibiting ethical behavior falls not only on the leaders of a company, but to all employees, managers, executives, and owners in

:qual fashion. When we look at the social laws that our society requires us to follow (man made laws), we need to recognize that these all stem (or should stem) from common law and ultimately from the ideals of Natural Law.

Constituent service in action

In 1997, the automotive supplier Donnelly Corporation made a presentation to the Work in America Institute defining the modern application of service to constituents. In that presentation, the full concept of what organizational service to others means was discussed: "(W)e define ourselves as a company...not just as some products, buildings, and employees who work in them. We comprise the sum of our shareholders, our customers, our employees, our suppliers, and our communities. We believe that our company exists to serve all the people who are members of these groups. This is partnership."[20] This perspective has, at its foundation, the necessity to understand and to practice ethical behavior.

> *Most of us tend to think that the best business practices must only occur at the largest companies, and probably those with a "traditional" corporate model. This, however, is not the case.*

It's easy to dismiss these ideas as "feel good" fluff, and something that really doesn't work in the real business world. In 1992, the Donnelly CEO, Dr. Dwane Baumgardner, reflected on the business reality of the "fluff" this way, "It requires a solid understanding that our past

---

[20] *"The Greatest Reward for a Person's Work: Manufacturing Fit for Human Habitation"*, Paul Doyle & Carol Kaplan, Work in America Institute, September 12, 1997, pg. 4.

performance and past relationships are not good enough in today's environment. Competition is out there trying to knock us off. It requires a singular responsibility that we hold all members of our team accountable and it requires us to face a challenge to make this need believable, and relevant to us. If we don't do all of this, then we can't say that we have integrity. Integrity also involves owning the process and having a genuine interest in becoming what we have never become before as this relates to our personal, professional, and organizational aspects of our work."[21] Dr. Baumgardner wasn't deceived by a lack of recognition of the competitive realities of the market place, but he understood a different reality of how to be successful in that market place.

Structure doesn't matter – substance does!

In Chapter 1, I referred to an *Economist* article that showcased the kind of companies that exhibited the greatest level of service performance – those that are closely held with outside advisors. What the article didn't say is what the company structure of these star performers was. Most of us tend to think that the best business practices must only occur at the largest companies, and probably those with a "traditional" corporate model. This, however, is not the case. Any company size with any company structure can be a star service and ethical performer.

Each year, *Fortune* magazine comes out with its "100 Best Companies to Work For"[22] feature. While this view looks primarily at the satisfaction and benefits for employees, it is probably a good barometer of the company's overall service to its constituents. In 2004,

---

[21] Dwane Baumgardner, Speech made to Scanlon Conference, May 27, 1992, pg 7 (slide 9 notes).

[22] *Fortune Magazine*, December 2003.

the top 10 included J.M. Smucker, legal services firm Alston & Bird, Container Store, financial services firm Edward Jones, Republic Bancorp, Adobe, engineering and construction company TDIndustries, software maker SAS Institute, family-owned supermarket Wegmans Food Markets, and chipmaker Xilinx. Most of us probably only know 2 or 3 of these top 10. These companies aren't the largest or most well-known in the world, but they all offered a different view of what operating a successful business means. In describing the #1 company in the U.S. to work for, *Fortune* described J.M. Smucker as "throwback to a simpler time." According to *Fortune*, employees said the company treats them like family, with a corporate culture based on objectives including: "Listen with your full attention, look for the good in others, have a sense of humor, and say thank you for a job well done."[23]

I was recently listening to a lecture by Randy Gage in which he commented that a home based business starts every six (6) seconds in the U.S..[24] That's a lot of folks trying to do for themselves something they can't find in the traditional business world. Most of these new start-ups include an affiliation with some sort of MLM (multi-level-marketing), network marketing, direct sales, or *Peer-to-Peer© Business Model.*

The initial reaction of most business professionals to this kind of business is one of contempt. However, somehow, these businesses continue to be successful. One such company is the Irvine California based Arbonne International. The company is a skin care and health care company founded by Petter Mørck in 1975. Based upon skincare formulations developed at the corporate labs in Switzerland, the company

---

[23] From: http://money.cnn.com/2003/12/29/news/economy/fortune_bestcompanies/

[24] Randy Gage, *Escape the Rate Race* – CD Lecture, 2003.

is recognized as one of the most successful in the industry. Arbonne's current president, Rita Davenport, was once an entry-level consultant. Her success and that of the company is based on an extremely high level of moral and ethical behavior. Many of Arbonne's Regional and National Vice Presidents not only openly recognize the significance of service as a critical element of their business, but also work with their "down-line teams" to ensure this "tradition" continues with the growth of the company. Arbonne's website describes their success this way:

> *"The wonderful thing about Arbonne is that it's not just about great products, it's also about great people. The Arbonne family is made up of thousands of individuals working to make their dreams come true. Through sales incentives and rewards, travel opportunities, a generous SuccessPlan and great products, Arbonne offers a unique opportunity that can help make anyone's vision for the future a reality."[25]*

While this statement is certainly a marketing spin to put the company in the best light, the reality of it is often attested to by the independent consultants and Arbonne clients.

Questions to consider[26]

1) What does service to constituents mean?

---

[25]http://www.arbonne.com/the_company/the_company.htm

[26] It is important to remember that the illustrations used throughout this chapter and throughout the book are to put into context an example of the issues described. These illustrations however do not provide sufficient argumentation to draw specific conclusions, although they may point to these conclusions. Drawing conclusions from limited examples is a logical fallacy called "from the specific to the general." See:
http://www.logicalfallacies.info/presumption/hasty-generalisation/ for more definition of logical fallacies.

2) How can business benefit from adopting a "service" perspective?

3) Are our beliefs toward serving reflected in our business actions?

4) Do I recognize the basis for my personal business behavior?

5) How do I model and encourage service behavior in my company?

Interview with Dr. J. Dwane Baumgardner, PhD.

Baumgardner, a resident of Holland, MI, joined Donnelly Corporation in 1969. With his technical background and a Ph. D in Engineering, Baumgardner led Donnelly's technology team until he was named President in 1980. In 1983 he became President/CEO, and in 1985 he also began serving as Chairman of Donnelly's Board of Directors. When Donnelly was acquired by Magna in 2001, Baumgardner continued to serve as the Vice Chairman and President of Magna Donnelly until his retirement in September, 2003. Under Baumgardner's direction, Donnelly, and later, Magna Donnelly, experienced an extremely successful period of business growth in excess of 3000%. Dr. Baumgardner is a member of the Board of Directors for the Scanlon Foundation; a member of the Board of Directors of SL Industries; a member of the Board of Directors for Landscape Forms; and also a member of the Seidman College of Business Board of Advisors. Dr. Baumgardner is co-author of the book, *The Leadership Roadmap: People, Lean and Innovation.*

Q.)   For those unfamiliar with the concept of "constituents", can you describe what this means and what their importance is?

A.)   Essentially, what a company *is* is a collection of the needs of constituents. Each of the 5 constituents has critical needs, and the role of any company is to bring them all together. All of these needs must be simultaneously met if a company is to be strong. All the greatest companies are regularly meeting the needs of its constituents. While at Donnelly, we established "the mandate", which essentially was a quantitative statement of what the company must accomplish to keep all the stakeholders or constituents working together. This mandate and its practice by the stakeholders has to be willingly and enthusiastically for it to be successful. In a world of competing opportunities, there is no way to be a consistently high performer without the attention to constituent needs.

Q.)   In your role at Donnelly you came into a company that had already adopted the importance of constituents through the initiatives of John Donnelly, Sr.. How did this environment influence your business style and you personally?

A.)   The fact that this type of business practice was in place was part of the decision in joining the company. Specifically, the importance of people and teams was why I wanted to join the company. Donnelly was a special place, and had the most concise coherent principles ever written. I've always seen myself as a servant leader, and this business style made my job easier.

Q.)   How difficult was it for you as CEO to balance the sometimes conflicting needs of the various constituents? Are there any particular situations that stand out in your mind?

A.)   My primary role is to lead in a way to meet the needs of all. Often the objectives seem out of balance, but that is distinguishing between short term needs versus total needs. The situation that stands out the most is the unrelenting demands of the OEMs (original equipment manufacturers) on price and therefore on profit. Here the biggest single pressure is reflecting the needs of the company's shareholders and employee growth. This issue seems unique to the domestic OEM's. While companies like Toyota and Honda have demands, they also possess the ability to build partnerships that are good for both parties.

Q.)   You often hear skeptics suggest that things like business ethics and constituent service are naïve in the "real" business world. What would you say to those skeptics?

A.)   I would tell the skeptics, and anyone else, "don't fool yourself". Without ethics and service you are not going to be around long, either personally or professionally. Look at companies who have failed and you can see why. There is no doubt in my mind that performance and longevity are directly linked to the personal and professional ethics by which a company operates.

Q.)   Sometimes the "enlightened ways of doing business are more dependent on a person than on its integration into a business culture. Did you have any experience like this when you left MagnaDonnelly? How do you really institutionalize something like serving constituents or adopting ethical business practices?

A.)   Well, the way to institutionalize is by building business systems based on a solid business philosophy. An example of this was/is the "equity system" put in place at Donnelly. While this is separate and distinct from work structure, it is critical to the success of the company through recognizing the importance of the employee. This system continues to serve the new company in a largely unchanged way. Part of the due diligence that we took in evaluating the acquisition by Magna was to ensure the compatibility of the values in bringing the company together. I believe that both sides felt this ethical alignment was good and that the combination of companies would be a positive experience. We were/are confident that all the constituents would continue to be served well considering the market. The issues I've seen in the loss of some of the service culture are not due to a mismatch between the companies (Donnelly and

Magna) but due to and shaped by individual leaders in each of the groups. These really are because of the peculiarities of the individuals not knowing or not caring about the culture in place, and the importance to the constituent.

Chapter Three – Workers, the First Constituent

Us vs. them

Throughout different parts of our society, we have seen and continue to see many areas of life with an "us versus them" attitude. Racial conflict, class warfare, and labor disputes are easily recognized examples. All of these can be said to stem from not accepting the golden rule, or simply not listening to our inner voice about fairness and ethics. While some of these issues are based on the perceptions of reality instead of true reality, the basis for us vs. them in labor disputes is based upon real abuse – on both sides. American history classes have taught students about the late 19th and early 20th century mistreatment of employees, the difficult working conditions, and the unsafe conditions to which workers had to respond.

> *This constituent was viewed more often than not as one that needed to be tolerated, not served.*

Out of these employee "abuses", a social backlash occurred through the rise of traditional union activities. The benefit brought to the employees was often overshadowed by the violent actions of both the employers and the employee unions. While the movement institutionalized the idea of employee benefits and "fair" treatment, it also resulted in the stark "us vs. them" approach to daily business interactions. Unions "forced" employers to recognize their employees as a constituent. However, this constituent was viewed more often than not as one that needed to be tolerated, not served.

All of us, at some time in our lives, probably have been an employee somewhere; some in small business, others in large companies, still others in public service like government or education. Our experience may have been good or bad, but in either case, taught us much about the relationship between employer and employee. Our latest generations probably don't remember the "blood, sweat, and tears" which many think was necessary to get us to where we are today.

Changing the view

During the middle of the 20th century, a different view regarding employee importance and contribution began to emerge. It was a steel worker and union activist named Joseph Scanlon who worked to develop the concept of equity and participation in the work environment. The importance of Joe Scanlon wasn't in who he was or where he came from, but in what his work did for workers across the country and around the world. Where European and socialist workers "rights" continue to exist in a hostile and adversarial relationship with employers, Scanlon practices are designed to highlight the critical interdependence between employer and employee. These theories and practices recognize the service to constituents of workers *and* owners, along with the moral and ethical foundations that underlie the behavior of each.

Ultimately, Scanlon's work was developed further by Dr. Carl Frost of Michigan State University, into 4 basic areas: 1) worker and organizational identity and education; 2) employee participation and responsibility; 3) employee and employer equity and accountability; and 4) individual and organizational commitment and competence. The efforts of Scanlon and Frost have the ability to create, "organizational effectiveness while promoting individual growth and responsibility. It enables management to create a rational working environment in which each employee's dignity is recognized and every employee's potential is challenged in achieving the organization's objectives."[27]

Quoting from Harvard business review, "Scanlon believed that the typical organization did not elicit the full potential from employees, either as individuals or as a group. He did not feel that the commonly held concept that the "boss is boss and a worker works" was a proper basis for stimulating the interest of employees in company problems; rather, he felt such a concept reinforced employees' beliefs that there was an "enemy" somewhere above them in the hierarchy and that a cautious suspicion should be maintained at all times. He felt that employee interest and contribution could best be stimulated by providing the employee with a maximum amount of information and data concerning company problems and successes, and by soliciting his contribution as to how he felt the problem might best be solved and job best done. Thus the Scanlon Plan is a common sharing between management and employees of problems, goals, and ideas."[28]

The dignity of work

While not consciously articulating the religious basis in the development of work equity,[29] Joe Scanlon did understand the impact of personal dignity and professional ethics in business. Employees can

---

[27] http://www.scanlonassociates.org/Scanlon/ScanlonWebSite/home.html

[28] Lesieur, F. G., and E. S. Puckett. "The Scanlon Plan Has Proved Itself." Harvard Business Review, September 1969

[29] Scanlon's personal view on the religious basis of equity has been described to more closely representing a "secular humanist" view of society. While Scanlon was an Irish Catholic, there is little evidence of this being the primary driver of his work, according to Paul Davis, President of Scanlon Leadership Network.

be treated with dignity, possess the freedom to grow and reach full potential, and be held responsible for their performance. In our generation, religions and religious leaders around the world are more actively involved in the ideas of social justice, including workers rights. In the church document, *Laborem exercens (On Human Work)*, the rights of workers are included within the sense of broader human rights. Not only are the rights of workers to be championed, but so too is the *dignity* of the workers.[30] Dignity is not just in the work itself, but also dignity in the treatment of those working - in a manner pleasing to God!

> *Employees can be treated with dignity, possess the freedom to grow and reach full potential, <u>and</u> be held responsible for their performance.*

The "manner" that is pleasing to God are the behaviors that follow "the golden rule" and treat employees as employers want to be treated; view employees as constituents to be served; and are consistent with natural and revealed law of God. Natural and revealed law don't simply control individual behavior through a set of dictates, but provide for the dignity and full potential (in God) of humanity. Here again, the mix of ethical precepts point to and fulfill natural law. The golden rule is an example of social contract which has become a deontological command; "do onto others" becomes "thou *shalt* do unto others.

It doesn't matter whether one looks at the Christian or other religious tradition - scripture, the church and its religious leaders generally say that freedom is not removed from responsibility and responsibility is not contrary to dignity. Saying it again - in the setting of

---

[30] *Laborem exercens*, John Paul II, LE 9 & LE 16, Paulist Press, 1981

business, employees can be treated with dignity, possess the freedom to grow and reach full potential, _and_ be held responsible for their performance.

Living the corporate example

More often than not, we hear about the bad treatment of workers, or how employers fail to care for the well-being of the workers. In fact, Chapter 4 will delve deeper into exactly these kinds of failures – but here I want to share an example of a company initiating the call to service of its employees, even its extended employees.

In May of 2004, Gap Incorporated released the findings of its internal investigation on the working conditions of its employees around the world.[31] Gap wasn't required to do the study; it wasn't under any consumer or government scrutiny; and it had no compelling financial interest in the event the results came out poorly. Like most other apparel companies, Gap actually produces only a small portion of its own products (if any) and contracts the construction of its merchandise to contractors around the world. Most of the contractors are in emerging market regions such as China, India, Central and South America, and Africa. The global apparel industry is driven by intense price competition making it "necessary" to operate in these regions where practices toward employees are suspect and often abusive.

---

[31] "*Gap's New Look: The See-Through*", Fast Company, September 2004, pgs. 69- 72.

> *Following its "ethical sourcing" efforts, Gap removed business from 136 of its contractors' factories, and refused sourcing to 100 others when they could not meet Gap's labor standards.*

What Gap found was the widespread mistreatment of its contractors' employees, not only with respect to pay and working conditions but also physical and psychological abuse. The results of the Gap study weren't especially surprising given the nature of the industry, but what was surprising is how Gap handled the findings. The most significant action by Gap was to go public with the details of the working conditions of its contractors' employees (its extended employees). The second was that Gap actually took proactive steps against the contractors. Following its "ethical sourcing" efforts, Gap removed business from 136 of its contractors' factories, and refused sourcing to 100 others when they could not meet Gap's labor standards.

Although its actions aren't necessarily the same as changing its own employee conditions, the impact in removing its products may very well have a significant effect on its suppliers' treatment of employees, and perhaps also have an industry wide effect. The road for Gap to arrive at this action wasn't always a smooth one in which they willingly made the changes – in fact, the release of this report came only after a shareholder resolution was filed. The lesson here, however, is that Gap has recognized the importance of service to employees around the world.

Recognizing the authority of the boss

For the employer, ethical behavior and moral corporate action toward employees must embody dignity, freedom and accountability, but it does not mean a handing over of ultimate responsibility.

Managers, as representatives of the employer, must accept these duties as part of their job within a company. Participation by employees in all areas of work life, agreement of what these activities are, and performance attainment are all necessary elements that must be managed. However, the manager must always recognize his/her responsibility in service of the employer and not confuse participation with anarchy, or consensus with unanimity.

Most of us have had a boss that we looked at and thought, "How can an idiot like that be *my* manager?" Accepting the authority of the person we work for is the employees' part of service and moral behavior. Although we may believe that we should be our boss's manager, they have been placed above us for a reason – not just the reasons of business, but also by the design of God. We may not understand it or like it, but we need to be willing to accept it. Like the pre-existence of natural law and the authority on which it is based, so too does the boss possess the authority. While the temporal authority may come from the employer, the moral authority comes from God – "Let everyone obey the authorities that are over them, for there is not authority except from God, and all authority that exists is established by God."[32] Whether or not the boss acknowledges their responsibility from God, it exists and requires moral and ethical behavior because of it. "As a consequence, the man who opposes authority rebels against the ordinance of God; those who resist shall draw condemnation down upon themselves."[33]

In my own life, I have been employee and employer, worker and manager. Struggling to accept the direction of others has been more

---

[32]Rom. 13, 1, *New American Bible*, Catholic Edition, Thomas Nelson Publisher,

[33] Rom. 13, 2, NAB

difficult than trying to provide the participative leadership. Believing that I was being treated with dignity was more difficult than believing I was treating others with dignity. In reflection, both beliefs were probably wrong. I was unable to recognize the moral basis for the treatment I received because I was unable to acknowledge or accept the authority on which the "boss" was empowered. Understanding the divine basis for being placed into particular positions of responsibility and authority over others has allowed me to understand that it is not by either my own purpose as a business owner or that appointed to me by my employer that my responsibility stems. The way in which I guide, direct, and treat my employees should be in a fashion honoring God - through honoring, valuing, and teaching my employees.

> ***They have been placed above us for a reason – not just the reasons of business, but also by the design of God.***

Religious tradition and teachings tell us that we are but vessels through which the goodness of God can work. Our service *as* employees and *toward* employees is based on this concept when viewed as one of morality and ethics. One mystical religious tradition that speaks of humanity as vessels for God is the Jewish practice of Kabbalah. The 18th century Jewish Kabbalist, Dov Baer[34] writes, "Imagine yourself as Ayin (nothingness) and forget yourself totally. Then you can transcend time, arising to the world of thought, where all is equal: life and death, ocean and dry land. Such is not the case if you are attached to the material

---

[34] *Maggid Devarav le-Ya'aqov*, ed. Rivka Schatz-Uffenheimer, pg. 186, Jerusalem: Magnes Press, 1976 – as referenced in: *The Essential Kabbalah: The Heart of Jewish Mysticism*, Daniel C. Matt, pg 71, Castle Books, 1997.

nature of the world. If you think of yourself as something, then God cannot clothe himself in you, for God is infinite. No vessel can contain God, unless you think of yourself as Ayin (nothingness)." The point of including this here is not to create some idea of a mystical business philosophy, but simply to recognize that our effectiveness as leaders is increased when we allow ourselves to accept and apply the standards of God in our business behavior.

Questions to consider

1) As an employee, do you recognize your responsibility to your boss and employer; AND do you recognize the moral authority of those who are placed in management above you – regardless of your personal feelings toward their capability?

2) As an employer, do you recognize your responsibility to your employees; AND do you recognize your ethical and moral responsibility in treating them in a manner pleasing to God?

3) How can employers and employees use information sharing and decision making strategies to attain better business performance?

4) Do I operate as an employee or employer with a "changed view", or is it "me versus them"?

5) How do I model and encourage work and worker dignity in my company?

Interview with James Fellowes

Jamie Fellowes is CEO of Fellowes, Inc., a business that his grandfather began in 1917 with a simple records storage box, which he called a Bankers Box. Fellowes is one of Chicago's largest family businesses. Jamie worked alongside his father in his early career. He later forged a successful partnership with his brother, Peter, whom he recruited from higher education. Three years ago, his son John joined the company and now heads marketing for the paper shredder division.

From a base of just $4 million in sales and about 100 employees when Jamie joined the business in 1970, the company expects to reach in excess of $700 million in sales with its 1400 employees worldwide. Fellowes has broadened its product line to include personal and general office shredders, laminating and binding machines, and a host of accessories that are used around PC's, laptops, PDA's, and cell phones. Fellowes operates 13 subsidiaries around the globe and exports to over 100 countries.

Q)   Fellowes appears to take a very personal view of its employees. How much difference do you believe this view and treatment has meant to Fellowes and its employees?

A)   We do take a personal interest in our people. Each week I meet one-on-one with a few people from our organization with whom I would not have much contact in order to get to know them and allow them to know me. I find it valuable to know something about each of our people who make an impact on our business. We practice an egalitarian business style – avoiding hierarchy, privileges and perks. We all travel the same class: coach. We award reserved parking based on seniority, not title. We do little things to demonstrate our respect for the value and dignity of all people. We believe in simple ways of rewarding the human spirit. We want to create a work environment that aligns with the personal values of our people. We believe that people work more creatively and effectively if they feel valued.

Q)   As the CEO your visions and perspective about the critical nature of employees are very obvious. How do you ensure that your management team - from executive to entry level managers - share and implement this vision?

A)   The great challenge for all business leaders is to get the company's people aligned in vision, strategies, and values. Let's face it, we're all individuals and we like our individuality. We come from very different life experiences, diverse background, and culture. Little wonder that businesses often lack consistency. At Fellowes, we created a core ideology piece 'Fellowes Forward' which captures our core values, our envisioned future and key strategic themes. We integrate this ideology into the business to the extent we can imagine. We use it as a basis of the way we set strategies and goals, the way we communicate, and the way we measure and reward. Though Fellowes is a global company with many moving parts, 'Fellowes Forward' helps those parts move more gracefully together. Hiring the right people is critical. We screen our people rigorously to find people who share our values. We are not looking for diversity in values! We also identify core skills for all Fellowes people to make sure we are hiring people that fit with the requirements and style of our business.

Q)   Does the company, as a whole, view employees as critical constituents in the same way it would consider its customers and owners?

A)   The heart of our strategy is about people – even more so than the products we create, the processes which produce them, and the customers who use them. Why is that? We have learned that unless you have the right people in the right positions and in an environment which promotes their creativity and productivity, the rest of it never happens. In other words, the great products never get designed. The streamlined processes never are created. Customers never get thrilled by the value that is presented to them. In recent times we have invested increasingly on developing and enabling our people and bringing greater intentionality in shaping our culture and work environment. It is the key to innovation and success.

Q)   Do Fellowes' employees return the ethical vision to the company? Do they understand that the supervisors and managers are truly representatives of the owners?

A)   I believe that most people want to come to work and do what is ethically right. When top leadership is sounding the trumpet of ethical practices and then acting in accordance with the principles, most will honor and value the beliefs. Business integrity is one of our four core values. We define business integrity as keeping our promises, doing what is right, and being honest with ourselves. That defines a pretty tight triangle of principles to guide behavior. The key is making sure company leaders are falling inside this triangle with their decisions, directions, and behavior.

Q)   Can you highlight an example where your employees have taken a strong ethical stand?

A)   This past summer, while on vacation, I received a phone call from our Chief Operating Officer that we might be looking at a recall of one of our best selling products. Traces of potentially harmful benzene were discovered by a German regulatory group in a routine examination. As soon as we learned this, a decision was made to halt all shipments worldwide – a radical action, not called for by the German agency. But, it was the right thing to do. When I learned of this stoppage, a week later, we already had angry customers demanding shipment and fining us for shipping incomplete orders. For three weeks we nevertheless conducted a series of tests through several independent laboratories. Fortunately, they all concluded that the products posed no risk to humans. This was good news as we had been putting a process in place for a worldwide recall, estimated at millions of dollars. As it was, the stoppage in shipments for three weeks proved costly with lost business and fines from customers. What is the lesson? This story demonstrates that ethical practices, even at great cost, will take hold in an organization. Our problem was learned by mid-level managers who brought the issue to officers of the company. Our leadership team did what was right, at whatever unknown cost, because they had confidence that the company would back them. Business leaders need to feel confident that the company really believes and is willing to practice what it preaches.

Chapter Four – The Owners

The owners' dilemma

One of the greatest aspects of our country is the entrepreneurial spirit that has enabled the unparalleled growth in industry and technology unseen anywhere else in the world. Independent men and women with an idea and drive, and often with little or no money, created businesses worth millions (or now even billions), employed thousands of people, and have improved the quality of life often for the entire world. While we embrace the idea of the entrepreneur, we don't seem to embrace the continued success of the business owner. Maybe that's due to company structures where the owner is some unknown group of shareholders. But then again maybe not, because we often see individual owners like Bill Gates vilified. Perhaps ultimately it is the personal behavior and performance of the owners or their management teams that impact how others view the "owner".

> *While we embrace the idea of the entrepreneur, we don't seem to embrace the continued success of the business owner.*

The skepticism is often deserved in what we see on TV or read in the newspapers about individual and company behavior. Because of these revelations, we begin to think that our businesses and business leaders all must be corrupt. Otherwise, how is it possible that we see all the business failures and criminal prosecution that seem to be in every nightly news broadcast? Are the business owners really that corrupt and naive? And, if this is really the case, should anyone be concerned about the welfare and performance of business other than the owners themselves?

Why do we expect more?

Most business professionals see this disdain for what they do and how they perform and simply shake their heads. They just don't understand why they are expected to do anything other than what they are doing or to behave any differently. They believe that the "rest of the world" just doesn't get it. In reality, it may be they who just don't understand. There is a greater responsibility that needs to be accepted.

Douglas Smith is a leader in management thought about corporate behavior and a former McKinsey Consulting executive. Smith has been considered a "guru" of management thought. [35] In his recent book, *On Value and Values: Thinking Differently About We in an Age of Me*, [36] Smith describes a new role for corporations in the fabric of American life. Whereas in previous generations, culture and values was shaped by the attitudes and expectations of family, church, friends, etc., our current culture finds its values shaped by the business organizations to which we belong. According to Smith, our identification as individuals is now more driven by the question of "what do we do" versus "where do we live". Companies and company identity becomes the basis for individual identity.

---

[35] Smith & Katzenbach co-wrote the book *The Wisdom of Teams: Creating the High-Performance Organization* (Harvard Business School Press, 1993), considered a "classic" of business leadership thought.

[36] Douglas K. Smith, *On Value and Values: Thinking Differently About We in an Age of Me*, Financial Times Prentice Hall, 2004.

In a July 2004 analysis of Smith, Fast Company magazine writer Keith Hammonds distills the preparedness of companies for this new social responsibility to this one simple line – "Unfortunately, they're usually not up to the task."[37] Hammond describes Doug Smith's analysis of a shift in the community from "place to purpose" – the 'what do you do' from the 'where are you from' discussion. It is this shift that is profound and requires businesses and business leaders to accept a new level of social responsibility. There are few businesses and therefore business owners, who understand and accept this role.

Focused failure

When you consider the scandals of AIG, Sallie Mae, Bernie Madoff, Enron, WorldCom, Tyco, and all the others, you have to wonder what these failures have in common. I believe the reason that such abuses took place is that the single measure of success driving business and management performance was *the stock price*. It appears that it was only this measure of "shareholder value" (focusing on a single constituent) that drove the decisions in those companies. There is really no sense of social responsibility by the owners, only what Doug Smith describes as a "fundamentalism of near-religious obsession with the primacy of the investors."[38] Clearly many of these activities are not only lapses in ethical behavior or a lack of a moral compass; they too frequently are stark examples of illegal behavior. Once that line is crossed there is little doubt of the "rightness" of the behavior. Yet even

---

[37] Keith H. Hammonds, _We, Incorporated_, Fast Company, July 2004, pgs. 67-69.

[38] Hammond, _We, Incorporated_, pg. 68.

these illegal activities began with the first compromise of an individual's or group's moral belief.[39]

> *The executive and management teams then simply do what they are being "trained" to do – make any decision or take any steps necessary to improve the share price.*

So why does this happen? Because it is entirely likely that at these companies the most significant portion of executive compensation was based on stock price performance, paid through management bonuses. This indeed is the case in most executive pay structures, so what should we expect? The board of directors tells the executive management that they must deliver ever increasing stock prices; that their compensation is going to be based on stock price improvement; and ultimately, nothing much else matters. The executive and management teams then simply do what they are being "trained" to do – make any decision or take any steps necessary to improve the share price.

Clear evidence of this kind of "performance manipulation" for the purpose of bonus achievement was detailed in a September 2004 report from the Office of Federal Housing Oversight.[40] The report, *Report of Findings to Date: Special Examination of Fannie Mae* (September 17, 2004) stated that FNM "Inappropriately deferred $200 million of estimated expense in 1998, and established and executed a plan to record this

-----

[39] Similarly, there are many examples of legal activities which would violate a moral conscious. Exploitation of children is one such example, such as in legal child labor.

[40] Office of Federal Housing Oversight. The report, *Report of Findings to Date: Special Examination of Fannie Mae* (September 17, 2004). The document can be found at: http://www.ofheo.gov/media/pdf/FNMfindingstodate17sept04.pdf

expense in subsequent fiscal years. Furthermore, the deferral of such amount enabled management of the Enterprise to receive 100% of their annual bonus compensation. Without such deferral, no bonus would have been paid out."[41]

The report also said that "Fannie Mae compensation for executive officers involves several key components: 1) basic compensation, which includes base salary and other annual compensation; 2) Annual Incentive Plan (AIP) awards ("bonuses"), which link the size of the bonus pool to meeting annual earnings per share (EPS) goals; and 3) long-term incentive awards, which typically award substantial amounts of "performance shares" to executives if EPS and certain non-financial goals are met over a three-year period."[42]

Like most private sector businesses, FNM paid its executives the following (1998 payouts):

Officer	Title	Salary	Award/Bonus
James A. Johnson	Chairman and CEO	$966,000	$1,932,000
Franklin D. Raines	Chmn & CEO Desig.	$526,154	$1,109,589
Lawrence M. Small	President and COO	$783,839	$1,108,259
Jamie Gorelick	Vice-Chairman	$567,000	$779,625
J. Timothy Howard	EVP and CFO	$395,000	$493,750
Robert J. Levin	EVP, Housing	$395,000	$493,750

In every case, the bonus award based on EPS performance significantly exceeded the base salary for these executives. Because of the federal oversight of Fannie Mae, these abuses were discovered in the 2004 audit. Unfortunately, the bonuses were paid in 1998, so it took

[41] *Report of Findings to Date: Special Examination of Fannie Mae*, pg. 1.

[42] *Report of Findings to Date: Special Examination of Fannie Mae*, pg. 11.

nearly 6 years to discover this action. Private industry is unlikely to disclose these actions even with the increase in reporting under Sarbains-Oxley. Finally, the report stated "Notably, had net income available to common shareholders been reduced by $125 million, the EPS for 1998 would have fallen to $3.1127 - below the minimum payout threshold. As a result, no bonuses would have been awarded."[43]

Responsibility to the Owners

O.K., scandals notwithstanding, business owners and shareholders do possess a unique place in the company. When balanced with the requirements of the other company stakeholders, performance serving owners is critical. The performance, however, is NOT one of stock price but of revenue (sales) growth and profitability growth. It is these things that sustain momentum within a company's performance. Most investors and business owners know that stock price generally has very little to do with profitability and business growth. All we have to do is to look at the share prices of companies like Amazon.com to see this.[44] Stock prices are based upon supply and demand, often with emotion driving demand. When companies move away from stock price as a measure and embrace positive growth and profitability as measures of

---

[43] *Report of Findings to Date: Special Examination of Fannie Mae*, pg. 11-12.

[44] Amazon.com is a good example of this. In Oct 2004 Amazon was trading between $41 & $42/share with a P/E (price earnings ratio) of 63.7! This means that the stock was valued at 63.7 times its earnings, which until recently just prior had been losses – 2003 net profit $35m, 2002 net *loss* $149m, 2001 net *loss* $526m. The company has a stock value (market cap) of $16.9 billion but will earn only $363 million (EBITDA), and has a negative book value of $1.95/share. Data from: http://finance.yahoo.com/q/ta?s=AMZN & http://finance.yahoo.com/q/is?s=AMZN&annual as of 10/6/2004. On July 9, 2009, Amazon was trading over $78/share, its PE multiple lowered to about 50 since it had started making profits, but still clearly excessive multiple. The market cap had nearly doubled during this time, while annual net profit remains around 3% ($645k for year ending Dec 31, 2008).

owners' success, _sustained_ success can be achieved. Growth and profits become key elements, along with employee and customer performance.

> *When companies move away from stock price as a measure and embrace positive growth and profitability as measures of owners' success, sustained success can be achieved.*

Let's face it - there are a lot of things that employees don't really want to accept. One of those is that there should be profits for the owners. Although the owners take the financial risks providing the capital that sustains the business, most of us harbor some sort of envy or even resentment that someone else is going to make money off our efforts. But like the moral authority provided by God to those above us, so too is there a moral and religious responsibility to work to provide returns for the business owners.

In the biblical parable of the silver pieces, Jesus tells the story of a master who left his servants with pieces of silver, entrusting them to manage the money wisely. Upon his return, two of the servants had doubled their money, acting as good stewards of his trust. The third simply returned the master's money having been overly cautious and hiding the money instead of working with it. The "performance review" of the first two said that they were clever, industrious, and reliable – being invited to share their master's joy – maybe like profit sharing? The third, however, was described as a "worthless lazy lout", and was ordered to be thrown out[45] - he was fired! The workers fear about his performance and master's response was indeed borne out by his

---

[45] Matt. 25, 14-30,NAB

dismissal. Was it that the master expected that those he trusted to do his work would actually do it, or was it that he was a master to be feared? Perhaps the servant's fear and uncertainty he created his own self fulfilling prophecy in which the feared outcome came to be. How often does this occur with employees when their view of their employer anticipates the worst? The parable demonstrates the responsibility of employees toward their business owner – to make good use of the resources provided AND to make a profit. While the intention is to metaphorically speak about the responsibilities toward God in the spiritual and religious life, it can also be a literal story about how we should behave in business.

As employees, most people find themselves grudgingly putting in their time and punching the clock. Tradition even says that unhappiness in work is a punishment for Adam's disobedience to God.[46] Our duty is to perform our best in every role, for all responsibilities. In the story above, the performance of the first 'employee' was better than the second but the boss was happy with both because they showed initiative and care – AND made a profit. The third did nothing and was rightly criticized for it. But certainly it wasn't his fault – in fact he probably would criticize the first two for being "brown-nosers" and kissing up to the boss. All of us who are employed are called by God to be caretakers of those for whom we work. Our responsibility doesn't depend upon which role we find ourselves (i.e., employee, employer, parent, spouse, child, etc.). Our responsibility is to ethically and morally serve others in a way pleasing to God.

----

[46] Gen. 3, 17-19, NAB

Balancing responsibility

In Chapter 2, I discussed how God places his people in authority or subjugation of others for a specific purpose. Even in those cases where the employee feels the employer is not worthy of respect, *God requires a return to them.* Generally, my professional career has been in purchasing for major corporations. In those roles as a buyer, or manager, or executive, I came to see my responsibility as being the keeper of the security of the company's finances. My employer and the company owners expected that I would do everything that I could to manage the company money well, and help to keep the company profitable.

There were many times that I was responsible for hundreds of millions or even over a billion dollars of the company's funds. In managing this, I had to remember to balance my responsibility of leadership/authority toward employees and suppliers with my obligation to the owners. In a constituent-based company, there are often times when multiple responsibilities conflict with one another. Real leadership (not management, but leadership) comes from being able to balance these conflicting objectives without sacrificing the underlying basis for fair and ethical treatment of each constituent. Like leadership itself, accomplishing this balance isn't always easy or popular – but it is the right thing to do.

> *Real leadership (not management, but leadership) comes from being able to balance these conflicting objectives, without sacrificing the underlying basis for fair and ethical treatment of each constituent.*

Summary

It's not easy being an owner or serving an owner. There are far reaching responsibilities and obligations as both owner and employee.

As an owner, you must recognize the broader cultural responsibility that your company imparts to its employees. The way you think and behave will ultimately become the way your employees behave. As employees, there is a responsibility to provide the owners with a real return. In pursuing the daily responsibilities of employment, both owners (and their executive representatives) and employees are faced with competing objectives and ethical dilemmas. Our reaction to these dilemmas is the key determinant in how well we balance the service to owners in a moral and ethical way.

Questions to Consider

1) Is there really a shift in cultural identity from the community to the company and, if so, what does it mean to our traditional institutions?

2) Do you as a business leader/executive embody the moral leadership required in the way you run your business?

3) As a shareholder in a company, do you hold management accountable for ethical behavior or are you driven by stock price alone?

4) As an employee, do you feel that the owners are entitled to a profit? Is there a maximum they should get?

5) How do you recognize and balance competing or conflicting objectives?

Interview with Andy Yahraus

Andy Yahraus is CEO and owner of Modern Industries, Inc. Modern Industries is a $70-100 million aerospace and semiconductor equipment manufacturer. Founded by Andy's father Dan Yahraus, Modern Industries is seen as one of the leading equipment manufacturers in its industries.

Q)   Individual and family owners who also take an active role in the operations of a business face a unique challenge in balancing the expectations of the owner with the responsibilities of operating management. What do you find the biggest challenge to be in this regard?

A)   Probably the biggest challenge as an owner is the propensity to make the business into a philanthropic organization. The operating management side helps keep the philanthropic side in check. I personally view my role somewhat in the sense of what I call Catholic utilitarianism, that is, "what am I going to do with the 'bag of gold' that God has given me". By determining what and how I am going to use these gifts, directly translate into the success of the business. A better organization can be created; greater business growth can be achieved; other "good things" can be done in a responsible way.

Q)   How are you able to communicate your personal sense of business responsibility to your management team and employees, and how well do you see that carried through?

A)   Communicating responsibility begins by first modeling the behavior you would like to see in others. But we also have developed and use a tangible "symbol" of what our responsibilities are. We've created a pyramid of "foundations of responsibility" which provides for all of our employees the basis for what we do. Every employee is given a desktop version of the pyramid as a continual reminder of those beliefs. I've found that our long-term employees intimately understand our culture and the nature of our business and of ourselves. However, being in an industry that has dramatic expansion and contraction, we need to be able to quickly communicate these values to our new employees. I believe that providing this outward symbol helps in their understanding and engraining them in what we do and who we are. Dr. John Sack from Arizona State University was tremendously insightful in helping us create this symbol. You can never be fully sure that the responsibilities and values you hold don't lose something in the translation from level to level. However, to try to keep as "true" as possible, our company makes no differentiation of rank and file employees and managers regarding responsibilities. Everyone is held accountable (including me) to the company foundations, while dealing with the realities of business. Every employee at all levels is encouraged to bring concerns directly to me if they find that the company or individuals here are not upholding these foundations.

Q)   Owners are faced with competing demands from customers, employees, as well as their own. How do you recognize and balance these competing demands?

A)   We start with the fundamental core of these demands and build from there. There is and will be a hierarchy of demands. When the bell rings, you may have to move and focus somewhere else. Ultimately, we have to understand the "total life of an employee" to determine if we are doing the right things at the right time. As an example, we recognize that there will be competing demands of a single parent bumping up against the need to remain profitable, a customer versus employee conflict.

The only way to achieve a balance of these demands is through developing and retaining long-term employees. In everyone's lives there are times when we are non-productive due to life circumstances. By working with employees to "get to the other side" of life's debilitating issues, we can continually build bridges to where they are able to contribute to the other demands beyond themselves. I recognize that sometimes this work may include termination if necessary, but perhaps it's that seed that will ultimately grow.

Q)   Have you viewed your responsibility as Owner/CEO as one of primarily "business" focused, or one of social responsibility & morality - explain?

A)   My role is one of social responsibility and morality first. My role as a CEO is to figure out what talents I (and others) am given, and then how to make the world a better place by using them. Within our company, I ask the question of whether our people are better for working here – uniquely better, not just growth. By asking this, I have to also face the potential that some are worse off – if this is the case then I have a very big problem. Awareness is hugely powerful; whether it is my own awareness or the awareness of those who work here. Our view of morality is 100% non-denominational/ sectarian. I believe that there is tremendous importance in being uniquely open to follow ones' own theology. I need to help others to become aware of the morality and responsibility that each one of us possesses.

Figure 1 - Modern Industries Symbol of Values

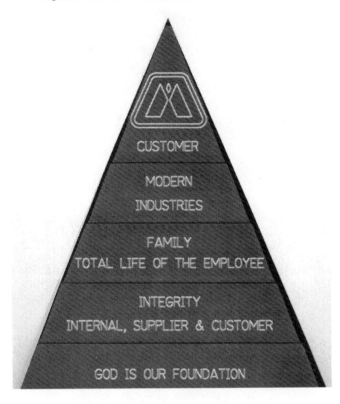

Chapter Five – The Customers

Let the buyer beware!

In ancient Rome, there was a popular phrase to describe contemporary business relationships; that phrase was: *Caveat Emptor!* - 'let the buyer beware.' It's the kind of thing that you should expect when you are at a street bazaar in a tourist town somewhere in the world, not as a standard of commerce. Let the buyer beware was the standard in the ancient commercial world. What the buyer had to be aware of was that there was no promise of good workmanship, no promise of safety or quality and no promise of getting what you paid for. Perhaps it was that there was little regulation of goods or maybe it was that there were no alternatives from where or from whom to buy. Whatever the case, we are fortunate that in our modern American marketplace we seem to be much more protected from many of these commercial concerns. But while we may no longer need to worry about the safety or quality of most products, we still are faced with an uncertain proposition with respect to being treated fairly – especially in the industrial marketplace.

In modern consumer and industrial business, customer focus is often one of the primary measures of successful performance. Goals are established around customer service; mission statements are written around customer satisfaction; and individual performance is often measured with regard to customer focus. There are now companies who make their living doing nothing else other than measuring and reporting customer satisfaction. One of these companies is J.D. Power and Associates. J.D. Power awards for satisfaction and quality have become the "Nobel prize" of customer satisfaction and are extensively used in product marketing. The J.D. Power corporate home page provides direct consumer reporting as well as a corporate site targeting information gathering and reporting.[47]

However, while most companies claim to understand the importance of maintaining satisfied customers and the critical need to service customers, many businesses act in complete contradiction to this belief. We see this in the way many retail and financial companies[48] will pursue every avenue to push up prices and costs, preying on the naiveté of unknowing or uneducated customers. Often, the product or services promised fall far short of the expected performance. Businesses frequently fail to stand behind the product or service they provide, going back to the days of caveat emptor – again, 'let the buyer beware'!

> *However, while most companies claim to understand the importance of maintaining satisfied customers and the critical need to service customers, many businesses act in complete contradiction to this belief.*

Jeffrey Gitomer writes in his book, *Customer Satisfaction Is Worthless, Customer Loyalty Is Priceless : How to Make Customers Love You,*

---

[47] http://www.jdpower.com/index.asp. One such report is the *CSI* (Consumer Satisfaction Index) *Power* that is described as "a quarterly publication that presents the best practices, key drivers and analysis of customer satisfaction across industries, based on data of J.D. Power and Associates. Included are the issues particular to individual industries. The publication also features the many factors and processes that can help improve customer satisfaction in all fields", found at http://www.jdpower.com/library/publications/index.asp.

[48] In the class action lawsuit Roberts v. Fleet Bank, Fleet Bank was charged with fraudulently and unilaterally changing "fixed" interest rate credit card terms to variable rates, violating the federal Truth-in-Lending Act. While denying that it violated any laws or did anything wrong, Fleet Bank has agreed to a $4.0 million settlement to the case. Case 00-CV-6142, Philadelphia, PA. Settlement details available at: www.aprsettlement.com.

Keep Them Coming Back and Tell Everyone They Know, a very stark assessment of his view of the performance to customers. Gitomer believes that the present relationship between most companies and their customers is ugly and not getting any better. He describes it as: bad and getting worse, with the bigger the company the worse the service; that companies continue to distance themselves from their customers; that customer service training is centered around company policies, but customers don't care about policies – they care about service; that employees care about themselves and not the customers or company; and that customer service people are not prepared to service in a memorable way, but only to the lowest acceptable level.[49] Now maybe Gitomer's view is a little pessimistic, but then again it may actually reflect how many customers feel towards the companies they are "forced" to do business with. In an arm wrestling match concerning "poor" customer service, Gitomer himself was barred from flying USAir because of how vocally he expressed his displeasure with the lack of service.

Philosophy of commercial justice

The sales and marketing executives of today may not recognize that their zeal to gain lifelong loyal customers is not made possible by slick marketing campaigns or misleading sales tricks, but really made possible by adopting the corporate ideals of commercial justice. Commercial justice is really no more than institutionalized ethical treatment of customers in the market place. It is not squeezing out every possible

---

[49] Jeffrey Gitomer, *Customer Satisfaction is Worthless, Customer Loyalty is Priceless: How to Make Customers Love You, Keep Them Coming Back and Tell Everyone They Know,* pg. 27, Bard Press (TX), 1998.

dime of profit today, but one of building relationships for tomorrow. Possessing the sense of "fair play" provides the greatest opportunity for developing a loyal customer base. This applies both to companies and individual products as well. In fact, ethical behavior can even provide for a second chance when a company responds in the "right way". Johnson & Johnson was able to accomplish this when it immediately pulled all its Tylenol products from the shelf in the early 1980s after reports of cyanide poisoning and deaths from product tampering.[50] Because of its immediate and honest response, its customers remained loyal to the product when it was reintroduced. Johnson & Johnson and Tylenol were given a second chance.

But fair and ethical treatment of customers is not only a good idea for continued business success and customer loyalty, it also reflects individual and corporate maturity. However, this individual and corporate maturity is based on enlightened views toward service and responsibility. Describing enlightened views of corporate maturity sometimes makes me laugh in that treating customers in an ethical way has been a social and religious philosophy for thousands of years. How enlightened can something be that is 3,000 or 4,000 years old! We readily see this idea of commercial and personal responsibility in ancient Jewish and Babylonian[51] writings. In the ancient Hebrew teachings, the Jewish people are told to be "true and just" in their

---

[50] In 1982 and 1986 cyanide-laced Tylenol capsule were discovered, defining "Market-Place Terrorism." In response to the incidents, Johnson & Johnson, the makers of Tylenol, immediately pulled all of its product from the shelves, ultimately replacing them with tamper resistant packaging. This action has been considered a breakthrough approach, and saved Tylenol's market reputation. See: www.facsnet.org/tools/ref_tutor/tampering/backgr.php3.

[51] George S. Clason, *The Richest Man in Babylon*, New American Library – Penguin Putnam, Inc., N.Y., N.Y., 1988.

business dealings and that "anyone who is dishonest in any of these matters is an abomination to the Lord....".[52] They are also warned against taking advantage of others in price, or by cheating them in goods provided.[53] Unfortunately, in the few thousand years of spiritual direction and coaching, many people and businesses in our society have failed to embrace these rules of business.

> *But fair and ethical treatment of customers is not only a good idea for continued business success and customer loyalty, it also reflects individual and corporate maturity.*

Justifying behavior

In the hectic pace of daily business, it becomes a very easy proposition to "justify" questionable behavior towards customers. I would guess that every one of us has experienced either individuals or groups within a company who explain away any misdeed as either deserved or as justice for some perceived wrong. Perhaps we have done it ourselves. Most of these justifications somehow involve money. I once worked for an employer that believed fully in its position of "cheating" one of its customers out of tens of thousands of dollars. The company had accrued money that was known to be owed to the customer. The customer was notified two or three times that the money was owed to them, but they never processed the adjustment. Finally, my company simply decided to keep the money instead of pursuing the credit. Although the company knew that the funds were not its own and would have endlessly pursued its own reimbursement, it felt no moral

[52] Dt. 25, 13-16, *The Catholic Study Bible*, New American Bible, Oxford University Press, 1990.
[53] Am. 8, 4-6, NAB

obligation to ensure repayment to the customer – it justified its own actions to serve the outcome. I'm not sure which part of this story is the most personally alarming - the fact that this occurred at one of my employers or that as an executive at the company I didn't do anything, although I knew it took place!

The leap from ethical to blatantly unethical behavior occurs in very small increments. In the story above, the company had been facing financial challenges and was making the appropriate internal changes to reduce cost and improve profit. Each step along the way seemed reasonable when compared to the one just prior to it. It is only when the totality of the gap is examined that the true impact of loss of moral direction is discovered. This is often the case businesses encounter when they examine the relationship they have with their customers. The "natural" response from the customer is a similar pushback and justification of its own behavior, perpetuating the cycle of moral degradation. Since the customer had been pushing us in a seemingly uncaring and unrelenting way, a decision was made to do the same – while feeling no remorse about it.

> *The leap from ethical to blatantly unethical behavior occurs in very small incremental steps.*

The power of intention

Customers can often be seen as naive and gullible, but in reality are probably far more perceptive than they are given credit for. We can "feel" whether the salesman we are working with is trustworthy or a "snake". Our gut tells us that the company we are dealing with is good or bad. The words and actions of the "snake" may be exactly t. the good guy, but somehow we just know. Dr. Wayne Dye known and respected author and lecturer who specializes in po empowerment,[54] attributes this sense of knowing to the intention of the person (or company) providing the product or service. In his book, *The Power of Intention,*[55] Dr. Dyer defines intention more than just the intellectual or cognitive criteria that decisions and actions are based on. To Dyer, intention is the spiritual motivation on which action is based or, more accurately, intention is consistent with the abundance of the Creator. If the intention that action is based on is consistent with God, your action is "on purpose". When business actions are "on purpose" with the intention of God, that is ethically-based, the results will show and customers will respond accordingly. Dyer describes those people who act on intention with others as "Connectors". He says, "All you have to do to tap into the power of intention is to be in a perfect match with the Source of everything, and I'm choosing to be as closely aligned with that Source as I can."[56] I interpret this in our words for business as Dyer saying that when we, as individuals and companies, align our efforts with the moral and ethical behaviors that are universally, spiritually and religiously required, our outcomes will be in perfect harmony with our intention. This is the complete opposite of what we all know as "gigo" (garbage in, garbage out). This really is gold in, gold out!

---

[54] Information regarding Dr. Dyer is available at: http://www.drwaynedyer.com/home/bio.cfm

[55] Dr. Wayne Dyer, *The Power of Intention: Learning to Co-create Your World Your Way*, Chapter 1, Hay House Inc., Carlsbad, CA., 2004.

[56] Dyer, *The Power of Intention*, pg 247.

But, business success is often viewed as existing in an ultra-competitive world with little or no time to consider the spiritual or ethical intentions that drive actions. Nevertheless, many of the most successful businessmen and businesswomen possess a very different attitude and believe in the spiritual nature of intention. Among those is Marvin Bower, former managing director of McKinsey & Company. McKinsey & Co. is often considered the founder of professional management consulting,[57] and Bower was one of its leaders. Although management consulting is frequently a segment of the business world that is considered among the most abusive, under Bower, McKinsey adopted a corporate policy that the clients' interests must come before the company's. For Bower and McKinsey, no consulting engagement was to be taken unless the value to the client exceeded the fee charged.[58] It was the intention of the company that drove its behavior, and its behavior that drove the satisfaction to its customers. With this, Bower provided the ethical leadership in which action toward the client had the importance of "the golden rule".

Being a good customer

Part of the problem of customer satisfaction efforts is that sometimes customers get what they deserve. Well, perhaps not, but customers do have a responsibility to offer the same ethical and moral behavior as they expect. Jeffrey Gitomer's problem with USAir was that his displeasure went too far and he failed to be a good customer. Instead of focusing on the issues, he became part of the problem by

---

[57] Maxwell, *There's No Such Thing as Business Ethics*, pg. 48.

[58] "A Profession is Born: 1930s," Our History, McKinsey & Company, www.mckinsey.com, February 10, 2003.

taking out the issues personally on the people he was dealing with. Likewise, in one of his early books,[59] Wayne Dyer said that if you wanted to get something resolved, remember that "a clerk is a jerk". Now his intent wasn't that the individuals in clerk positions were jerks, just that they couldn't really provide any meaningful solutions. Both recognized the problem and made their own mea culpa.

Seldom, if ever, do we consider the behavior of a customer as an ethical encounter. Americans, in fact, tend to cling to an egocentric version of the view that "the customer is always right." There fails to be the recognition that most customer transactions take place in a commercial setting not in the retail setting. That is, for every consumer transaction there exist multiple business to business transactions. Because of these factors, it can be difficult to imagine the way in which faith comes into play in the moral conscious and ethical behavior of a customer.

Nevertheless, religious precepts actually [can] play a powerful role in defining the "proper" attitude and behavior when acting as a customer. In Christian religious tradition, it could be said that in a sense Jesus provided great customer service,[60] even while often having "bad" customers. He was called on to provide for his "customers" and even when he provided beyond what these "customers" had ever hoped for, they tended to fail on their end of the bargain. Consider for

---

[59] Wayne Dyer, *Pulling Your Own Strings*, HarperTorch (1994).

[60] There is somewhat of a difficult transition to make here since Jesus was not in business but in ministry. Additionally, he often "broke to rules" of good social behavior with his affiliations, and snubbing of cultural codes. Overturning the tables in the temple or "calling out" Jewish leaders and teachers as hypocrites or simply as stupid wouldn't qualify for good customer service.

example the healing of the leper in Mark chapter 1 (and the 10 lepers in Luke chapter 17).

"A leper came to him (and kneeling down) begged him and said, "If you wish, you can make me clean." Moved with pity, he stretched out his hand, touched him, and said to him, "I do will it. Be made clean." The leprosy left him immediately, and he was made clean. Then, warning him sternly, he dismissed him at once. Then he said to him, "See that you tell no one anything, but go, show yourself to the priest and offer for your cleansing what Moses prescribed; that will be proof for them." The man went away and began to publicize the whole matter. He spread the report abroad so that it was impossible for Jesus to enter a town openly. He remained outside in deserted places, and people kept coming to him from everywhere."[61]

You may be asking, really? What could this possibly have to do with customer behavior? Consider for a second that the person of Jesus is seen in an individual or company which provides exclusive services or products to its customers. Part of that service includes an agreement of confidentiality, so that the service or product remains proprietary. Most readers of this scripture passage may simply smile and believe that Jesus wanted the news of his healing to become widely known. But that is not what we read. The cured man's lack of living up to his end of the bargain resulted in Jesus being unable to travel freely.

In our modern world, many times when customers fail their end of the bargain the results are much more destructive. Technologies can be lost, services stolen, individuals besmirched, and/or companies being put out of business. Chapter 6 will specifically address customer actions

---

[61] NAB, Mk 1, 40-45. In Lk 17, 11-18, after curing 10 Lepers, only one returned to give thanks.

towards suppliers; still it is important here to recognize the impact of customer actions - actions that result in either positive or negative "customer management."

Consider the response in the healing of the 10 in Luke 17. There were 9 Jews and 1 Samaritan healed of leprosy. Again, the charge to the healed was to say nothing and present themselves to the priests. Certainly healers weren't uncommon in ancient Palestine and Galilee. Perhaps in fact, the Jews of the day expected this type of "service" to be available. The story in Luke however, demonstrates an interesting aspect of human nature – appreciation and gratitude; or better said, the lack of appreciation. Nine of the ten failed to recognize, or at least acknowledged, the magnitude of what they had just received – as a gift no less.

Most of us want to believe that at the core of human nature is the capacity to be thankful and appreciative of what we have and towards those who have provided for us. As customers, we frequently forget or suppress this "natural capacity" for gratitude. Many feel that since they are paying or somehow "deserve" what they are receiving, thanks is not necessary. Many parts of our country are clearly guiltier of this than others.

Returning a moment to the Luke healing story; in a plot twist, it is the Samaritan who returns and gives thanks. In ancient Judea, a Samaritan would be a customer typically hated by the Jews, and one who would likely return that hate. Yet it is he and not the fellow countrymen who are thankful.

"Ten were cleansed, were they not? Where are the other nine? Has none but this foreigner returned to give thanks to God?" Then he said to him, "Stand up and go; your faith has saved you."[62]

We see in this story that it is often those that we least expect who are the most gracious and appreciative.

But again, why is this important? In a tenuous way, these stories reflect the fragility of human nature and the human condition, while reinforcing the ideal we are called to in the tenets and examples of faith. When we receive bad customer service we are often easily offended; yet many don't give their own bad customer behavior a second thought. This behavior is even more exaggerated when one considers the magnitude and velocity of commercial transactions. Both customers and suppliers alike essentially create the conditions they will experience in business transactions. The intention one possesses as a customer, and even the expectation they have on how they will be treated tends to be what they encounter. More often than not, in business transactions the intention is to "win" no matter what the cost – fairness, appreciation, and ethics are often very distant concerns.

Sometimes you need help

Finally, in this chapter, I want to tell a personal story of simultaneously good and poor customer service, and good and poor customer response in a single experience. In November 2003, my wife and I purchased a new Buick Rendezvous. The vehicle had all the bells and whistles, On-Star©, DVD player, heads-up display, the works. In August of 2004, my wife and 6-year-old son were across the state returning from a family funeral. My wife called me in the office and said

---

[62] Luke 17:17-19.

that the air conditioner had just shut off and there was a little smoke coming from the front passenger side. I told her that she should pull off as soon as she could, call On-Star, and tell them the problem and get away from the car.

She was able to pull over within a couple of minutes and, while finding her a way off the highway, she contacted On-Star and told them the problem. Here's where the first poor customer satisfaction came in – the operator at On-Star told my wife that she needed to put her on hold for 3 or 4 minutes. Unfortunately, before the 3 or 4 minutes were over, my wife and son were out of the vehicle which was now totally engulfed in flames. After the event, I contacted On-Star and explained my concern and asked them to investigate the response. I was trying to be a good customer, but still wait for that reply!

We then were faced with the task of trying to get some sort of settlement for the vehicle. We filed all the necessary reports, contacted everyone we were supposed to, but waited and waited – for over three months. Initially, we were told that we would receive the fair market value of the vehicle ($15,000 less than what we had paid 8 months earlier) for the "thermal event" we experienced. This is where I became the "bad" customer, losing all patience in response to the poor customer service. Fortunately, the cooler head of my wife prevailed. While we both wondered what happened to the full "bumper to bumper warranty", my wife was far more patient in waiting than I was.

> *Instead of treating customers like a valued constituent, customers are viewed with skeptical pessimism.*

Ultimately, we had the vehicle replaced to an amount we could all agree on. Undoubtedly, this amount was probably what we all knew it should be, but Buick "blew it" by losing what could have been a lifelong customer. Had we been able to reach the same settlement 2 or 3 months earlier, Buick probably would have had a customer for life, as we would have told everyone how well and fairly we had been treated. Instead, they have me tell the world what a rotten job they did. The cooler head of my wife thinks they did a great job. Her intention was one of patience and she ultimately got exactly what she wanted. She is very happy with the outcome and has no complaints about the process. I think that part of my frustration was that in working with the GM claims and accounting areas, they seemed to feel no sense of urgency or need for customer satisfaction. To me, everyone I spoke to was part of customer service and they performed pretty poorly.

As in this story, companies often snatch defeat from the jaws of victory. Instead of treating customers like a valued constituent, customers are viewed with skeptical pessimism. The intention of mistrust comes back in a response of mistrust. The intention of only winning comes back with the result of winning the battle but losing the war. Ultimately, when the intention of corporate behavior is customer service through ethical action and moral behavior, success is more likely to occur.

Questions to Consider

1) Is your view of customer service one of "making the surveys look good" or is it truly one of service to a valued constituent?

2) Are the needs and expectations of your customers known in your organization or are your satisfaction efforts based on your company policies alone?

3) Are all your employees prepared to provide "service in a memorable way" or "only to the lowest acceptable level"?

4) Does the concept of "commercial justice" have any meaning in the products or services that you provide or is it caveat emptor?

5) Are you a good customer who encourages others to value you and your business relationship?

6) In providing or receiving products and services, how does your individual and company intention match up with the results you hope to achieve?

7) How many times has your performance, or lack of performance, caused you to "snatch defeat from the jaws of victory"?

Interview with Jeffrey Gitomer

Jeffrey Gitomer is the author of *The Sales Bible*, and *Customer Satisfaction is Worthless, Customer Loyalty is Priceless* as well as other leading titles relating to customer satisfaction and service. Jeffrey gives seminars, runs annual sales meetings, and conducts training programs on selling and customer service. He has presented an average of 120 seminars a year for the past ten years.

His syndicated column, *Sales Moves,* appears in more than 90 business newspapers, and is read by more than 4 million people every week. His three WOW websites ~ *www.gitomer.com, www.trainone.com,* and *www.knowsuccess.com* get as many as 5,000 hits a day from readers and seminar attendees. His state of the art web-presence and e-commerce ability has set the standard among peers, and has won huge praise and acceptance from customers.

Jeffrey's customers include: Coca-Cola, BNC Mortgage Inc., Cingular Wireless, Hilton, Choice Hotels, Enterprise Rent-A-Car, Cintas, Milliken, NCR, Financial Times, Turner Broadcasting, Comcast Cable, Time Warner Cable, Ingram Micro, Wells Fargo Bank, Mercedes Benz, Baptist Health Care, Blue Cross Blue Shield, Hyatt Hotels, Carlsburg Beer, Wausau Insurance, Northwestern Mutual, A.C. Nielsen, IBM, AT&T, and hundreds of others.

This interview is a summary taken from a lengthy phone interview October 28, 2004.

Q.)   Many companies will have a corporate philosophy statement or some other expression of what they do to satisfy customers. However, when you look at what most really do, it seems that very little is done to satisfy the customers. How would you explain this?

A.) Management vision of a mission statement is often 180° from their actual practices. If they are looking to exceed customer expectations, then why would they say "please select from the following nine options to serve you better?" But that's all what I refer to as self service not customer service. Self service is, "I'm going to do everything I can to cover myself, at the expense of everyone else."

Q.) What would you select as an example of this lack of customer service behavior?

A.) The classic model of this would be the airline industry or even the automotive industry. Both of these are high profile industries, but you can see that Delta just cut 10,000 jobs and reduced their schedule. But did they increase their service? Are you going to see a brand new airline at Delta? We've got wireless connections in the sky, have you seen that? No, you know why? Because their business is upside down! But it's a typical example of how they won't go to service, they just cut cost. No more blankets, no more pillows, no more bottles of water. A bottle of water in exchange for an $852 ticket! Come on, sell me the food, I'll buy it; sell me the water, I'll buy it. My God, not only have they eliminated essentials and reduced customer service, but they've also cut their employees pay as well. How well is a disgruntled employee going to provide service to the customers?

Q.) So if companies aren't focusing on the customer, then what are they focusing on?

A.) Most big companies talk about shareholder value which is the single dumbest move on the planet. What it means is that they willing to rape and pillage my entire company for the sake of a few bucks. They're willing to fire 10,000 people, cut services to their customers, shorten their hours, reduce their schedules, go to automated everything, and stop providing the services their customers are used to, all in the name of shareholder value. I think it was Warren Buffet that said "no company ever recovered by cutting costs." At some point you have to increase sales; at some point you've got to increase service to attract sales.

Q.)   There seems to be differences in how retail customers are treated (better) and how industrial customers are treated (worse). How can you change that mindset?

A.)   It's really a huge answer, but the first piece is obviously leadership. It's got to trickle down from the top. The boss has to show benevolence toward it and an attitude towards service not towards cost cutting. If they do cut costs, let the boss be in the middle of it. Let the boss be the first to take the cut. Chief executives are out there saying that they won't take a salary for the next year, but they've got a $20 million golden handcuff program. If they leave, they walk away with half the business. You don't see executives offering their golden program to be divided by the employees. So it's the ethics of omission. It's self service again. I find these actions deplorable. I find that they just won't come clean; just won't be honest, just won't be forthright. Ethics can't be institutionalized unless they start out with it from an orientation standpoint – and that piece comes from the owner or CEO. There are some places that just do the right thing all the time. When they do the right thing, they do fine. They make money. There are plenty of companies that do the right thing; unfortunately there are plenty that don't.

Chapter Six – The Suppliers

The other side of the coin

We all hate suppliers! Well maybe hate is a little harsh....we all despise suppliers! There's no doubt that they are out to cheat us every chance they get! Without constant management, they will undoubtedly screw things up!

O.K., how many of you believe or have said some of the things above? We know that as a buyer we need to beware of what we are going to get from our suppliers (remember Chapter 5?). But, unless we are the final retail consumer, all businesses are suppliers to someone. Are you an untrustworthy or unethical supplier? From a business perspective, the supplier is simply the other side of the customer coin. For every customer, there is a supplier and for every supplier, a customer. Everything we said in Chapter 5 about the appropriate behavior from and toward a customer applies here. There's only one small difference - as a customer, we expect to be treated well; as a supplier, we can expect to often be treated poorly.

The guidelines on ethical treatment towards customers apply likewise to suppliers. It is intriguing that the businesses which complain the loudest about the manner of treatment from their customers are the very ones who insist on treating their suppliers in the same way. If our ethical behavior does not exceed that which we criticize coming from others, how morally correct are we within our own business? Back to our biblical principles, Jesus taught that the greatest law is to behave the way in which you expect others to behave, treat them as you want them to treat you, and do it not for your own recognition.[63] While the treatment received from customers can only be influenced (not controlled) by the treatment given to them, the ethical behavior exhibited and the moral treatment of suppliers is *entirely* within the business' control.

> *There's only one small difference - as a customer, we expect to be treated well; as a supplier, we can expect to often be treated poorly.*

Confrontation versus collaboration

Most of the things that businesses buy are not retail but industrial purchases. These business-to-business (B2B) transactions are based on an interdependent need between customer and supplier. However, when push comes to shove, most large industrial buyers simply let their suppliers fall on the sword alone.[64] In their efforts to structure the most favorable purchase conditions, most large industrial customers insist on risk sharing, including provisions for annualized price reductions, warranty sharing beyond product replacement, and other similar risk factors. In an effort to protect themselves, most suppliers are now

---

[63] Matt. 22, 34-40; 23, 23-31, NAB

[64] Automotive News Article, " ***Specter of Bankruptcy Court Hovers:*** *Suppliers Under Siege"* from October 8, 2001, described the continuing business failures caused by the OEM's unrelenting pressure in pricing, warranty and other charge-backs without regard for business sustainability. While this article is now quite old, the practices have not changed and continued to be reported on. Similar situations continue to happen in the electronics and semiconductor industry where second and third tier suppliers are financially ruined by their customers' failure to honor purchase order and pricing agreements.

seeking warranty liability insurance. Unfortunately, many insurers (such as AIG) now refuse to provide this type of coverage in many industries. While the idea of risk sharing appears to be a reasonable requirement, its market application usually is one of ruthless blame transfer to the smaller or weaker supplier. In most industrial markets, with most customers, there is a very clear confrontational approach to supplier relationships.

Not all relationships need to be this way, however. Many companies have demonstrated the ability to create collaborative relationships with their suppliers that provide for a mutually beneficial business relationship, operating clearly within the expectations of ethical behavior. In an August 2002 article for Optimize Magazine, I addressed this with the following:[65]

> Accept that competing self-interests are the basis of the customer-supplier relationship. Buyer and supplier both consider their own stakeholder needs and present them as the starting point of the buy-sell arrangement.
>
> Establish customer and supplier objectives and, most important, metrics for success. These metrics, which might measure cost/price, design, quality, or other factors, become the objective basis on which the value of the relationship is measured.

My point is a simple one: working ethically with your suppliers relies on accepting the "collective fate" that you share. Collaboration may mean working with "the enemy", but it also means cooperating to

---

[65] Optimize Magazine, *"Competitive Partnerships"*, Jeffrey Wincel, August 1, 2002, pg. 40-44

achieve the desired result. Winning the battle doesn't always mean winning the war – ethics require us to share the victories outside the battles of the war.

The power of ethics

Most individuals and companies view their relationships with suppliers as confrontational because they can't see any other way to win. Also, they can't see winning unless someone else loses. Part of the problem is that in business, power is seen as control, not cooperation. When you control the situation, you control the outcome and you control the power! But power isn't coercive control; power is the ability to achieve a satisfactory result for everyone. Force is the coercive bullying ability to attempt to get what you want. However, force results in a Newtonian resistance – for every action there is an equal and opposite reaction. The more force you apply to your suppliers, the more force they apply back. Ultimately, each side is going to be applying as much force as possible, even to the point of exhaustion, but no one is going to get anywhere!

> *But power isn't coercive control; power is the ability to achieve a satisfactory result for everyone.*

In the book *Lean Supply Chain Management: A Handbook for Strategic Procurement*, I included a chapter dedicated to the concept of ethical treatment toward suppliers. Chapter 3 of that book was entitled "Skill versus Force", and dealt with the idea that most buyers confuse their coercive force with positive skill. The use of "force" often lies outside the boundaries of ethical behavior. From that book:

"Dr. David R. Hawkins, in his book *Power vs. Force – The Hidden Determinants of Human Behavior*, describes the effects of these two influence methods on personal, professional, and commercial relationships. In his use of power, Dr. Hawkins writes that "power arises from meaning. It has to do with motive, and it has to do with principle."[66] In contrast to the positive aspects of ethics in power, force depends on the lowest basic behaviors, appealing to crass "influence" actions.[67] Like Isaac Newton's law of physics, force in commercial relationships have a counter force fighting against them, whereas positive power derived from ethical behavior "energizes, gives forth, supplies, and supports."[68] So the determining factors the SCM professionals need to examine in evaluating the ethics by which they interact professionally are the behaviors they exhibit."[69]

I included this reference to Dr. Hawkins because I believe it elegantly describes the nature of ethical relationships with suppliers when he says that "power arises from meaning." Power here is not used in a negative controlling sense, but in an ethical and moral sense. Hawkins continued with "It (power) has to do with motive, and it has to do with principle." Many business professionals and executive managers believe that any treatment of suppliers that is not dominating and controlling is one from that they cannot benefit. Hawkins proposes the contrary that true benefit and power come from relationships based on intention, motive and principle.

For a company to have moral and ethical relationships with its suppliers it MUST provide a relationship whereby power is used to

---

[66] David R. Hawkins, M.D., Ph.D., *Power vs. Force – The Hidden Determinants of Human Behavior*, (Carlsbad, CA., Hay House Inc., 1995), pg. 132.

[67] Hawkins, *Power vs. Force*, pg. 132-134.

[68] Hawkins, *Power vs. Force*, pg. 132-134.

[69] Jeffrey P. Wincel, *Lean Supply Chain Management: A Strategic Procurement Handbook*, (N.Y., N.Y., Productivity Press, 2004), pg. 35.

achieve an outcome that provides the greatest combination of return for both buyer and seller. Force is not an acceptable basis by which work is motivated and result pursued. Actions by everyone in the company with suppliers are as strong as the words that they use to describe their ethical behavior!

> *Many business professionals and executive managers believe that any treatment of suppliers that is not dominating and controlling is one that they cannot benefit from.*

Walking the talk

Like every discussion of ethics, riding your "high horse" in the public arena is easy when the discussion is theory only. The tough part is when the rubber meets the road, and you need to actually deal with the potentially competing outcomes between you and your suppliers. It is in the heat of the daily battle, being tempted to fall back into the pressure tactics, that the true character of a company is tested.

Of the major challenges I faced in my career as a business executive, the one that tested my "walk" the most, was the repeated demand to hold suppliers accountable in the same manner that we were held accountable by our customers. While on the face of it, the reasoning for our expectations of cost, quality and delivery performance from the suppliers was appropriate, the underlying agenda was to treat our suppliers as ruthlessly as we were being treated by some of our customers. Regardless of the objective information which showed that the most reliable supplier performance resulted from treating suppliers firmly but fairly, many corners of the company viewed a collaborative approach as a weak one, and unlikely to be successful.

The greatest companies in the world and the greatest leaders in those companies gain that status by unrelentingly maintaining their business actions as a direct reflection of their words. While it may not always be popular, it is the reason that these people and companies achieve almost mythical status. Jack Welch was once seen as a corporate raider, but ultimately seen as the epitome of the chief executive. In the world of supply chain management, men like Gene Richter from IBM/HP/Black & Decker, and Dave Nelson from Delphi/Deere & Co./Honda, represent the pinnacle of ethical supplier relations, as well as achieving significant business and financial improvements.[70]

> *The greatest companies in the world and the greatest leaders in those companies gain that status by unrelentingly maintaining their business actions as a direct reflection of their words.*

Trust matters

There is no doubt that ethical and reliable behavior results in increased trust and cooperation between suppliers and customers. Confrontational and threatening behavior only results in a sharp decline in trust of and service to customers. In a February 2003 article in Purchasing Magazine, writer David Hannon detailed the effects of the automotive "Big 3" war being waged on suppliers in the article: "Suppliers: Friend or Foe?". Stating the obvious, Hannon detailed the unrelenting and almost unscrupulous behavior of the purchasing organizations of the domestic U.S. car manufacturer's purchasing organizations contrasted to that of the Japanese transplants. Even

---

[70] Gene Richter was awarded 3 Purchasing Magazine's annual "Medal of Excellence" during his tenure at IBM, Hewlett Packard, and Black & Decker, Dave Nelson won 2 Medals of Excellence while at Honda and Deere & Company.

former divisions now independents, like Visteon Automotive, complained of the unreasonable demands. A study from Planning Perspectives of Birmingham, Michigan showed the extent to which our U.S. companies were no longer trusted by their suppliers:[71]

	Trust Level
General Motors	2.12
Ford Motor Co.	2.21
DaimlerChrysler AG	2.26
Nissan	2.63
Honda	3.32
Toyota	3.40
(Scale of 1-5 with 5 the highest	

To finish this chapter, all industries are seeing the effects of the lack of suppliers' trust coupled with unreasonable demands. Often, the result is suppliers refusing to bring the latest technologies to some of their customers, and even walking away from business. If these actions continue, American business is going to suffer and continue to lose ground to our foreign competition. From the Friend or Foe article:

"In December, tier one supplier Tower Automotive announced it would not bid on the contract it held to supply frames for the top-selling Ford Explorer simply because "the expected returns at (Ford's) targeted pricing levels did not meet our requirements," according to a statement from Tower. Tower's move sent a message through the supplier community that the breaking point had been reached. While a

---

[71] Purchasing Magazine, *"Suppliers: Friend or Foe?"*, David Hannon, February 6, 2003. Full article available at: http://www.manufacturing.net/pur/article/CA273552.html.

supplier electing not to bid on a contract may happen more often than noticed, Tower's public battle with Ford served as a rally cry for U.S. suppliers."

In 2009 GM succumbed to bankruptcy; but not just bankruptcy, it also lost its independence, now being majority owned by the U.S. and Canadian governments – 60% U.S. and 12% Canada. Similarly, Chrysler fell into bankruptcy orchestrated by the U.S. government, and is now owned by the Italian car maker Fiat. Certainly, the GM & Chrysler failures are far greater than simply its treatment towards their suppliers, customers or other constituents; yet they are potentially reflective of a general failure to act ethically in some very difficult situations. Decisions demanding strong moral leadership and ethical behavior were frequently sidestepped, pushing the consequences until some later day. That later day arrived with ferocity in 2009.

Questions to Consider

1) Very few organizations consider their suppliers anything more than a necessary nuisance. Do you share this view, or are your suppliers a valued constituent?

2) Are the business relationships forged with suppliers one of mutual benefit or one of necessity driven by price?

3) Organizational and financial success is often determined by the management of issues often outside your direct control. Procured materials are often in excess of 50% of C.O.G.S. (cost of goods sold). Are your suppliers used in a collaborative way to jointly manage successful outcomes to your business challenges?

4) How often has your organization complained about the treatment it received from its customer, and then demanded the same treatment of your suppliers?

5) Do you and/or your company "walk the talk" with respect to supplier relationships? What is the implication of this on your corporate or personal ethics and morals?

6) Are you trusted by your suppliers? What does the presence or absence of trust indicate about you and your company?

Interview with Charlotte Diener

Charlotte Diener is Vice President and General Manager at ON Semiconductor. Having directed a team of 80 business unit directors, engineers, marketers, and program managers, Charlotte led a business unit with sales in excess of $500 million. Her professional experience encompasses executive positions in some of the world's leading manufacturing companies. Charlotte answers questions on the nature of suppliers based on her experience in both supply chain management and general management. ON Semiconductor (NASDAQ: ONNN) is a leading global supplier of advanced semiconductors for sophisticated electronics application within the portable, wireless, computing, consumer, networking, automotive, and industrial end-product markets.

Q.)   You have had the opportunity to work for many Fortune 150 companies as both a purchasing/supply chain executive and a general manager. As you transitioned roles from a functional executive to a general manager, how did your view of the role of suppliers change?

A.)   When you work in Supply or Purchasing you are very focused on how suppliers strategically fit into the internal processes. How does the supplier support advanced engineering? Do they have the technical competence to help your staff design products to the cost, quality and functional targets? Can they support manufacturing? Do they have locations around the world where the company needs them? Can I get the cost reductions the company needs from them? Once I became a general manager that perspective changed. The first question always is: "Should we do this project at all?" GMs begin by looking at the market, and then at the opportunity cost of doing something. How does it fit into the portfolio? What position can be gained in the market from this product? Only after those questions are answered, do we even begin to question whether something should be engineered or manufactured in-house or externally. It's at that point that a GM begins to think about suppliers. I view suppliers today as an extension of the capabilities required to bring a product to market. If my company can't do it more effectively than an external company, then I think of the suppliers. Who can do this technically? Who will stay with us over the long-term? Who is most competitive? If things are working as they should be, the answers to all those supply questions can be found in purchasing working in cooperation with engineers, business directors and technology development. It's not at all that I believe suppliers don't warrant attention; it's just that the sphere of concern for the GM has expanded. It's been my experience in both jobs that the best suppliers are the ones that you don't hear from very much! They share their engineering roadmaps with your engineers, they assist in new designs, and they deliver to the right place at the right time and right cost. Usually, if I am involved in any one of these things, something isn't right in the relationship between the companies or the performance of the supplier. From the perspective of a GM, the supplier is truly a link in the chain that reaches from the raw materials through us to the customer and, ultimately, the consumer. In supply, I was often very focused on the side of the chain coming into the company. When it comes to ethics, there are certain foundational principles that exist between the customer and supplier no matter what position you have in the company. I think that in addition to the obvious (no bribery, no kickbacks, and no special gifts), there are others that are just as important. Those are:

- The supplier never oversells his capability. (If it's risky, tell the customer upfront!)

- Neither the customer nor the supplier compromise each other's technical information or IP. (If you need a competitive quote, get it without using the supplier's information!)

- Companies don't ask suppliers to do things when they aren't committed to a project or market.

Q.)   Many of the largest companies describe their relationships with suppliers as "partnerships", but most suppliers don't necessarily see it that way. Why do you think there is a disconnect in what the companies are saying and what the suppliers are seeing?

A.)   Many times a partnership disconnect comes from conflicting objectives within the customer. Purchasing is always struggling to meet the changing needs of the business. Sometimes, the business priorities are on new technologies and new products to market. Other times, they are focused heavily on cost reductions. These changing needs manifest themselves around behavior with the suppliers. Often the communications time lag leaves the supplier solving what the customer views as yesterday's problems. Unfortunately, some customers' management looks to suppliers to meet their budgets, and force initiatives or behaviors that they would never undertake internally. I am not implying that the customer sees this as an ethical dilemma, but it is. The internal pressure to meet the budget, to make the numbers, to exceed is very great in the US because we are so short-term focused in our financial markets. That lack of long-term view toward financial results makes it very difficult for customers to take a long-term view to the supplier partnership. A great example of this is the use of on-line auctions when the pricing power moves to the customer, but discussion of partnership when the delivery power moves to the supplier. There is also a power disconnect in partnerships. Obviously, the customer always has the most power since they are signing the check. Large customers who sign lots of checks have even greater power. At times, this corporate power is misused by buyers or others at the customer. I have heard many suppliers complain that buyers are telling them how to run their business and what they should be able to do with costs, but many buyers have never had to meet a payroll or worry about cash flow. Suppliers resent this perceived 'arrogance" and it affects communication and ultimately the view of the partnership. I have also seen some very ugly behavior that I call the "Blame Game". It is easier to blame the supplier than to accept responsibility or fix an internal process issue. I have even seen some instances where the blame was placed on the supplier, which then provided the organization with some time to fix their internal problem. These things are not the behavior of people engaged in a successful partnership. Lastly, many large Western companies haven't truly adopted "lean" principles, e.g., target costing or value analysis and value engineering. They are therefore always focused on this year's cost reductions. This leads to constant re-quoting and the belief that there's a better supplier out there. Many times an incumbent has to fight to hold business that they have engineered and serviced for years. But, as long as customers can ask new suppliers to take on the extra inventory or extra cost, and the supplier does, the partnership will remain one of convenience.

Q.)   In the roles that you have had, were suppliers ever viewed as "constituents", rising to the same status of importance as customers and owners?

A.)   I have rarely seen suppliers rising to the levels of a customer. Speaking as a General Manager, nothing is as important as a customer! They pay the bills. I have seen this tried at Ford with things such as the Minority Supplier Council or Electronics Supplier Council. Often, these initiatives were driven by purchasing and not an accepted part of an enterprise wide program, so they never really rose to the constituent level.

Q.)   There is a lot of professional and industry literature that describes a continuing hostility between U.S. based purchasing organizations and suppliers, but not in Japanese companies. What is it that the Japanese are able to do to gain supplier trust and support that the American companies are not?

A.)   The Japanese have a long history of working with other companies in an extended enterprise through the Kieritsu system. By definition, that is a long-term partnership because you always turned to your Kieritsu partner company first. Even today, Japanese customers will often quote suppliers outside the kieritsu to drive price down, but if a Kieritsu company meets it – business goes to them. That attitude has led them to have a long-term partnership mindset. I would also add that all the Asian cultures have a much longer term view than Americans. Their corporate policies reflect that and their relationship with suppliers reflects that too. Additionally, value engineering, or designing to a target cost, is real at Japanese companies. There is an openness and acceptance to lean and VA/VE. Americans are famous for NIH (not invented here). If the supplier says they can't meet the cost target with a given design, Americans will often look for another supplier. Target costing is real in Japanese companies. I believe the kieritsu system again plays a foundational role in this.

Chapter Seven – The Community

The ethics of stewardship

There is no other topic in business and labor that is more passionate and polarizing than the "outsourcing" of production and services to foreign countries. The immediate impact of these decisions is being felt across the country and around the world. But a discussion about the effect of these decisions and ultimately the responsibilities toward community can't begin without understanding the responsibility to the land itself. In most cases, the conscious treatment of the land and natural resources of a community aren't a business priority. Companies generally consider the natural resources they use as "bought and paid for". But this view is far from the truth. The land and its resources are common property, and any of its use should be viewed as a "loan" which must be repaid with interest.

> *Companies generally consider the natural resources they use as "bought and paid for."*

The basis of the community ownership for the land isn't from some tree-hugging do-gooder, but stems from the moral foundation of natural law. Communities are called to care for the resources they possess by the simple idea of self-preservation. Continuing to survive, and more importantly to thrive, depends upon having the necessary raw ingredients to allow the growth to occur. This community and company responsibility is called stewardship. From the spiritual and religious view of stewardship, stewardship of the land, the animals, the plants, and all

in the land has always been considered a gift from God.[72] As part
t gift, while humanity itself has been responsible for caring for its
natural resources, business too has a responsibility to care for the
community in which it exists. This responsibility, however, goes far
beyond simply caring for the land. It includes caring for the people of
the community; caring for the growth of the community; and caring for
the beauty of the community.

Signs of social responsibility

Although signs of social responsibility have appeared on the
corporate landscape, they are often window dressing designed for show.[73]
Alleged environmentally safe products and operations; the sponsorship of
a major league sports team or stadium; and other like actions supposedly
represent corporate participation in the community. However, the *lack of
substantive commitment* is often evidenced by community blight brought
about because of lack of care for the facilities and the land that businesses
occupy. The *lack of substantive commitment* is evidenced by the flight from
traditional local communities to "low-cost" labor areas around the world.
The *lack of substantive commitment* is evidenced by taking money out of the
community through tax incentives instead of investing in the social
infrastructure of the community.

---

[72] Gen. 1, 27-28, NAB

[73] An argument can be made that social responsibility is one area of business ethics that has
been attempted. The effectiveness and sustainability of these efforts might be questioned, but
certainly efforts have been made. Literature like the *Journal of Business Ethics* is dedicated to
material regarding corporate social responsibility.

> *The lack of substantive commitment is evidenced by taking money out of the community through tax incentives instead of investing in the social infrastructure of the community.*

Substantive commitment from business to local communities is not a "lost investment" or an un-recovered cost. In fact, in most cases, the investment in the community often results in a significant return to the company. This "community dividend" is much like the "peace dividend"[74] spoken of in world politics when unexpected resources and capital become available. In the book *On the Moral Foundation of the Universe: Theology, Cosmology, and Ethics*, Nancey Murphy and George Ellis describe the effects of the use of a "sharing ethic";[75] in essence, a community dividend:

"This pattern is part of the paradox of the kenotic ethic.[76] The result can be more positive, however: once the sharing ethic is in action, it may well be that the pie to be shared will in fact be larger – partly because others will be willing to contribute resources they otherwise would have kept to themselves, including their labor. The cooperative motivation to work hard (on behalf of all of us) is increased in this case; workers may be motivated to produce more

---

[74] The peace dividend refers to the resources, including capital (money), which become available when they no longer need to be allocated to the purpose of preventing war or keeping peace. These dividends can be used for other needs, including social needs. Likewise, the community dividend provides additional resources to be available for business, such as allowing them to expand, increasing productivity and output, etc.

[75] Nancey Murphy and George F.R. Ellis, *On the Moral Nature of the Universe: Theology, Cosmology and Ethics*, Fortress Press (Minneapolis, MN), 1996, pg. 127.

[76] Murphy & Ellis, pg1. Kenotic ethic is the "particular moral vision" defined by Murphy and Ellis which, as they describe it, is "supported 'from below' by evidence from the social and applied sciences, and 'from above' by theology".

when they see it as beneficial to their community as a whole rather than to some group ("bosses") to whom they have no particular allegiance."

The caring ethic and the community dividend are actions and results specific to each local community. Because of this, a "corporate solution" to community responsibility will never be successful. Corporate moral action demands that companies must tailor their actions specifically to the communities in which they reside. Anything less is nothing more than the "cookie cutter" view of ethics in action. The biblical letters of Paul to the different communities in the early Christian era demonstrates the unique nature and the individual care and feeding that is necessary for each to grow and thrive. Paul recognized the individual needs and challenges that the various communities exhibited, and applied moral guidance to aid them in their growth.

The local and regional communities in which businesses exist are not only the natural and human resources available to support the creation of the company product or service, but also the **primary consumers** for those products and services. In the early 1900s, Henry Ford created not only a revolution in production technology through the moving assembly line, but he also created an entire consumer economy by paying his employees far more than any other employer.[77] His dedication to his local community, Dearborn Michigan, created unparalleled regional growth that lasted nearly 100 years.

---

77 James P. Womack, Daniel T. Jones, Daniel Roos, The Machine that Changed the World, Harper Collins, 1991.

> *Corporate moral action demands that companies must tailor their actions specifically to the communities in which they reside.*

Low-cost regions

The modern global nature of business competition is now making any commitment to a local community a thing of the past. Many of the traditional industrialized economies (such as the U.S.) are rapidly moving from being industrial societies to being service societies.[78] Many companies fail to recognize the real and immediate correlation between the local employee and consumption of its products. Since there is no perceived connection, there has been a marked increase in the flight of business from these local communities to "low-cost" foreign regions (China, India, etc.). These moves create a false sense of business success by trading off short-term cost reductions (and resulting profit improvement) for the ultimate loss of consumer demand. Displaced employees will no longer create the demand for products that are now produced elsewhere, regardless of the price. In this regard, business must realize that the "right" business decision is not always the lowest cost business decision. There is a narrow-minded perspective that looks only at cost, not total value. Value includes cost, but also measures other factors with equal importance.

What is the most perplexing issue is that many foreign international corporations are opening new production facilities IN

---

[78] Many sociologists have defined the economic structure of the U.S. as a service economy and as such, the primary mode of commercial transaction is one of buying and selling services versus buying and selling of products.

THE U.S., while most U.S. companies are closing down and moving overseas![79] What is it that the "transplants" know that we don't? Is it that they recognize the connection between consumer local market demand and employment? Are foreign companies rediscovering Henry Ford's model and making it their own? How can they afford to "upsize" in local U.S. communities while everyone else is rushing to downsize?

It's O.K. to be there

Moving into or from any community is not itself good or bad, ethical or unethical. When growth, new business opportunities, or new markets are found, growth into those local communities (domestic or international) is a benefit for both the company and the community (this is what the transplants have learned). However, when no such new market is found and the move is simply one of building a better cost structure, business ethics and corporate morality are *the* main issue.

Behind every outsourcing or low-cost region decision, there is always a "compelling" story. But companies and their executives are fully aware of the structure of the local work force and compensation when they purchase new companies or locate business into an area. Through their evaluation and decision making processes, they also know of the market and pricing pressures they face from their customers when they made the decision to accept business. The mythological "Corporate Office" should also know its responsibility to the community and to the dedication that made the purchase a good

---

[79] Toyota Motor Company is now the 2nd largest producer of passenger vehicles in the world behind General Motors. Toyota announced it plans to build a new vehicle assembly plant in San Antonio, Texas. This plant, representing an $800 million in investment - see: http://www.toyota.com/about/operations/manufacturing/texas/index.html. Likewise Nissan Motors also completed construction of a vehicle assembly plant in Canton, Mississippi in 2003.

one. By moving production, these companies simply found the "easiest" way to fix their own mistakes – or, as we talked about previously, how to increase their bonuses.

> *While financial concerns are usually the basis to abandon a local area, companies often face no real financial performance risk – and many may even have experienced <u>record sales and earnings</u>.*

The community impact

When companies announce the outsourcing of operations to low-cost regions, communities feel helpless at the continued loss of jobs and loss of hope. In trying to make sense of why long-time community residents would do this, there always seems to be a discussion regarding the changing face of economics in business and the local area. Many business and political leaders viewed the decision as simply a smart business decision to a tough situation – and stand by and do nothing. It is unfortunate that there never seems to be any discussion of the ethics involved in these decisions. While it is true that the company management made a "good" business decision which affected part of its responsibility (its shareholders), it failed many other parts – its employees, its community, its suppliers, and often its customers.[80] While financial concerns are usually the basis to abandon a local area, companies often face no real financial performance risk – and many

---

[80] The country is ripe with anecdotal stories about customer service support being sourced off-shore to India or China where the language and cultural barriers result in a groundswell of dissatisfied customers due to poor customer service.

may even have experienced <u>record sales and earnings</u>.[81] Even when a company's financial performance creates a compelling motivation to relocate to low labor cost regions, it does not secure the success of the company nor its survivability; such is the case with General Motors.

The decisions are generally made to improve profits even more, and one likely to serve the personal financial rewards provided as bonuses to its executives (executive bonuses are often based on short-term profit improvements and share price changes, as highlighted in Chapter Four). However, those decision makers have taken money out of the pockets of their domestic customers, putting only a small portion into the workers' pockets in the low-cost areas, and a much larger portion into management's own pockets.

Every day, businessmen and businesswomen make decisions that in any other part of life would be considered ethically questionable. But, since these are business decisions, they seem to be accepted as okay. We should live in a community where we hold true the ideas of ethics and morality. We should insist on the same from the businesses within our communities – to practice good business ethics and corporate morality.

An activist solution

When faced with unacceptable working conditions in the early 1900s, labor organized into powerful unions that shaped the face of business for the next 70 years. Although the union activism of the past is gone, a new activism is emerging that will undoubtedly be as distasteful to corporate America as the union movement was. The

---

[81] Holland Sentinel, *"JCI Cutting 885 Jobs"*, by Lisa Ingraham & Robert Gold, March 30, 2004. This was the case when JCI (Johnson Controls Inc) announced its relocation of production from Holland Michigan to Ramos Arizpe Mexico, shortly after it announced record sales and earnings.

activist answer to stem community abandonment is neither in legislation to penalize nor in tax or financing incentives to stop it, but in demanding that businesses understand that their moral responsibilities are far greater than the shareholders (and stock price) alone.

The demands won't be made through work stoppages as in the past, but in shareholder voting. The union movements made possible employee ownership through stock-funded pension and retirement plans. These plans have shifted a significant percentage of ownership from the private market, with proxy votes controlled by the boards-of-directors, to employees with proxies potentially controlled by unions or even other private organizations. Through company ownership in 401k programs, displaced workers possess the shareholder right to question the decision of companies. Many groups and individuals have begun using that right at shareholder meetings to put forward motions regarding business ethics and corporate morality. Business executives need to recognize that communities and individuals are moving in the direction of this new corporate activism.

Co-Partnerships

Industry has always thrown around the term partnerships when describing its relationship with its customers, employees and suppliers. Those in industry however, share the not-so-secret knowledge that the typical relationship is anything but a partnership. The guy making the rules is going to be the one getting all the benefit. This is in part due to the fact that there really is no shared investment in the structure or reward that each party is going to get. This, however, can be different with community. In most cases, community and business leaders must and do come together to create systems whereby both benefit from relationships. While most often this comes in the form of governmental support, there are other ways in which this can exists.

> *Co-partnership requires at least the setting up of structures whereby owners and managers can be held accountable for decisions and policies.*

In contemporary Catholic thought on service to constituents, the *New Dictionary of Catholic Social Thought* describes a concept called "co-partnerships". "Co-partnerships take the form of a number of structured processes whereby those who work toward a common objective assume on the basis of their work activity an increased competence and responsibility in the policies and operation of the office, plant or form for the sake of mutual benefit. Co-partnership requires at least the setting up of structures whereby owners and managers can be held accountable for decisions and policies."[82] While this definition is not overly elegant for the average business person, and where it seems to generally focus on the relationship between owners and employees, the underlying premise of advancing the common good can equally apply to all the constituents, especially those structured for community. Business ethics and corporate morality have at their foundations the common good for the benefit of all.

The highs and lows of acting ethically

When squarely dealing with the competing challenges of *typical* business decisions versus *ethical* business decisions, we are often faced with what seems to be "no win" scenarios. We feel that we either compromise what we know is right for the good of the company, or potentially jeopardize our own future by doing what is ethically better.

---

[82] The *New Dictionary of Catholic Social Thought*, pg. 237, Judith A. Dwyer, editor, Liturgical Press, 1994

Fortunately, even the most difficult decisions can result in an unexpected outcome where even in the short-term everyone wins. The challenge is to be willing to take the risk in doing the "right" thing, and believing that the right outcome will occur in both the long and short-term.

I've personally experienced a number of these kinds of decisions. Early in my career, I was faced with the choice of easily achieving a great cost savings through changing suppliers to the lowest cost source (the *typical* business decision); or considering both the economic and social impact of to whom and how I would determine sourcing (the *ethical business decision).* The typical business decision would mean personal achievement and recognition, while the ethical decision meant lesser savings and probably uncertainty to others of my skill in business. As is usually the case, the typical business decision was the easiest to understand, explain, and quantify. The ethical business decision was more difficult to understand and explain, and the quantifying showed it to be more costly. The fact was that while either choice represented a significant financial improvement, the 2nd choice represented an even better *value* choice (and the right ethical choice). Convincing the executive management of this was a different story. It took many rounds of discussions to convince the management team of the wisdom of the recommendation. Eventually, however, I was able to obtain the reluctant approval from my managers that the lesser cost savings was indeed the better choice – but the approval would be this one time only.

> *Although the "points" I could have scored from the higher savings amount were lost, the personal reward of maintaining ethical behavior was immeasurable.*

Ultimately, the choice also proved to be the best financial decision when the new supplier had re-tooled the parts at its own cost prior to assuming the business. When the existing tools arrived, they were found to be poorly maintained and virtually unusable. The "lowest" <u>price</u> supplier had quoted an increase of thousands of dollars if new tooling had been required, and would have quickly become a much higher <u>cost</u> supplier. Part of the ethical decision included knowing that increasing the amount of business with the recommended supplier would enable it to maintain a presence in the small community in which it operated – ultimately saving several hundred production jobs. Although the "points" I could have scored from the higher savings amount were lost, the personal reward of maintaining ethical behavior was immeasurable. I was also given other chances by the management team to propose similar solutions. While I'd like to say that I always did what I knew to be right, I can only say that I *often* did what I knew to be right. Like everyone else, I also did things that were expected, without consideration for the ethics.

Not every experience, in fact probably not most experiences, will result in the outcomes described above. Invariably, the "downs" of ethically-based decisions come and then a little rain must fall. It certainly fell on me in late 2001. In the midst of the political turmoil brought about by September 11th and the resulting economic slowdown, I was one of many people around the country downsized for the sake of company survival. Regardless of who you are or why you lose a job, you reflect on what makes you an attractive candidate before others. I'm sure that things like compensation savings played a factor, but I also know that the stances I took on ethical issues in dealing with customers and suppliers was another key element.

I failed to fully understand the discomfort I brought to others in challenging the moral and ethical basis for their decisions. As a company executive, I made some of my peers (and superiors) uncomfortably conscious of the decisions they were making. My departure from the company provided a relief from facing tough questions, especially at a time when too many other tough questions were being asked. Where I had viewed my moral and ethical views on business a strength, those who were more powerful than I did not. The realization of this became more apparent when many of the ethically-based supplier and customer relationship methods I helped to implement were eliminated. As a result of that elimination, the expected "push back" from suppliers and customers occurred causing even more turmoil for the company.

Summary

Community responsibility is among the most difficult constituent obligations to understand. More often than not, businesses feel that they are the ones who should be served by being in a community, not the ones serving. After all, they are providing jobs, taxes, benefits, etc., so why shouldn't they be the 'chief'? But, the issue really isn't a matter of who's serving whom, but in embracing the responsibility for repaying the investment that the community has made in its land, resources, and labor.

Ethical responsibility for community has to permeate the company psyche starting from the local teams, and going, ultimately, to the corporate offices. Without this, business decisions will remain devoid of morally-based criteria. It is these criteria that are necessary to understand and measure the full impact of corporate decisions to shut down and relocate to low-cost regions; to acquire new domestic and international businesses; to expand into new international or local marketplaces; and are ultimately necessary to empower the constituent service to and from employees, customer, owners, and suppliers.

Questions to Consider

1) How does constituent service to community recognize the importance of the land and natural resources, and take shape without assuming the negative mystique of being a radical tree-hugging environmentalist? Is it even possible or important?

2) Does business really adopt the idea of community as a constituent, or is it simply a disposable resource?

3) Why does it appear so easy for domestic companies to simply pull up stakes and move to global low-cost regions? What do these moves mean for the stability of their customer base? And, under what conditions, are these moves ethically acceptable?

Interview with Dr. H. James Williams

Dr. H. James Williams serves as the Dean of the Seidman College of Business at Grand Valley State University, located in Grand Rapids, Michigan. His degrees include a B.S. in Accounting at North Carolina Central University; an M.B.A. in Accounting at the University of Wisconsin (Madison); a Ph.D. in Accounting at the University of Georgia (Athens); and a J.D. and LL.M. (Taxation) Degrees at Georgetown University Law Center. Dean Williams is also a Certified Public Accountant and a Certified Management Accountant, with a wealth of practical experiences, having worked in the public accounting profession and in the legal profession (as a corporate and tax lawyer).

Q.)   A university possesses a unique place in the community in which they reside. Local support would seem critical to the success of the university's purpose. How do you view the role of GVSU in serving the community?

A.)   GVSU shares a major responsibility to serve the West Michigan community, along with other businesses and organizations in the area. Our State charter suggests that we respond to the community's needs. Our role as an educational institution demands that we respond to the community's needs. Indeed, it occurs to me that in light of its founding by a group of business persons who perceived the community's need for a university of GVSU's breadth and depth, the University owes a special duty to respond to this community's needs. Of course, Seidman's competitive advantage in serving the community is through business and economic development services and support activities. The inherent challenge is to manage the service to the community in a manner that facilitates and promotes the

College's discharging effectively its main mission to educate the region's citizenry.

Q.)   How do you, as Dean, communicate your views and values of service to your academic and professional staff, and how do you insure that the vision is actually put into action? (or is this even done?)

A.)   My biggest mode of communication is by example. I try to live, on a day-to-day basis, my strong belief in service as a precursor to effective leadership. Moreover, I endeavor to communicate my points of view and perspectives to faculty, staff, and students on a regular basis. Finally, I try to share the "service to community" philosophy as often as an appropriate occasion arises. To facilitate communications, I send "Communications Memoranda" on a regular basis to the faculty and staff. I also encourage them to communicate to me their questions, concerns, and ideas - telephonically, via email, and face-to-face. I have also established student advisory boards at both the graduate and undergraduate levels to foster open and consistent communications between the students and myself. Finally, I visit classes on a regular basis to get to know students and I virtually never turn down an opportunity to speak to a student group or organization. I seek to assure that the "vision" is actually put into action by remaining aware and sensitive to the signs and signals. I talk with as many persons as I can and I listen as much as I can, to students, faculty, staff, community leaders, etc. I remain in a continuous-improvement mode at all times, which requires my critically evaluating whether we are achieving our goals.

Q.)   Working in a public university, it would seem that your ability to speak of ethics and morality is severely limited because of the prohibition (often legal)   of adopting anything other than a situational secular basis for ethics. With this in mind, are you faced with any difficulties in modeling your personal view in these areas versus the "allowable" view?

A.)   I do not feel at all inhibited in the basis I use for my own approach to ethics, which is anything but secular. Indeed, by law, there can be no interference by a State institution with that. On the other hand, I also cannot use the State's facilities and activities to try to convince someone else to adopt some type of religion-based approach to ethics decision-making. Still, I (and other faculty) have much latitude to discuss and promote dialogue of different religious-based approaches to ethics decision-making, as long as it is germane to the subject matter and not offered in a manner that implies State sanction or denigration of a particular religious tenet or approach. In fact, faculty members have a special "Academic Freedom" right to broach some of these topics where they are relevant to the subject matter, and not simply gratuitous. On the other hand, I speak of morality only in very broad terms and almost never in my teaching (primarily because it rarely is germane to the topic of accounting). In discussing ethics in accounting, on the other hand, I often speak of society's mores and how they impact our legal and value systems in ways that sometimes promote unethical behavior. I think there is plenty of latitude to discuss the full range of issues attendant to ethics, even in a State University. Moreover, I believe the Courts recognize and respect that latitude.

Q.)   How do you develop a curriculum and course material that speaks to the issue of ethics and morality? What are the challenges in doing this with a diversified student body?

A.)   I think, as with the development of any curriculum or course, we must begin by answering the question of what are we trying to achieve regarding the subject matter, in this instance "ethics and morality." More specifically, we must ask ourselves what we want our business graduates to either "be" or "be able to do" regarding ethics in the work place. Moreover, whatever we want to achieve must be achievable in the context of a college education (either at the undergraduate or graduate level). (I believe that business ethics, ultimately, is a function of personal morals and values. In fact, I believe that it is very difficult to shape someone's personal mores and values over a two or four-year period of time. Accordingly, at least in my opinion, it would be unrealistic to develop an ethics curriculum designed, at least ostensibly, to "teach the student ethics." Instead, the course or curriculum (in my opinion) ought to focus on making students aware of ethical dimensions and dilemmas in a business context.) The development process must begin at this step: determining what can be realistically delivered in the way of learning goals. The next step in the process is to translate those learning goals into measurable objectives; that is, when the student possesses the character trait or has achieved the learning we planned, how will he or she manifest it? Then, we must ask what readings, activities, exercises, discussions, exposures, etc. will best achieve the learning goals in ways that will manifest themselves as we project. The biggest challenge that a diversified student body presents is the "learning styles" and "standards of challenge" issues. Faculty must consider, at the outset, how a diversified student population affects the learning goals, the delivery of those learning goals, and the students' manifestations of the achievement of the learning goals. The different dimensions of diversity (race, economic, religious, age, and etc.) create their special learning challenges. Obviously, persons learn differently and at different rates of speed dependent upon their natural abilities and talents, as well as their socio-economic and other experiences and exposures. Heterogeneity of the student population has many tremendous advantages but also presents some tremendous teaching and learning challenges. Finally, an effective curriculum or course development process must include an assessment mechanism or process that leads to continuous improvement and refinement. I do not think the diversity issue causes any great challenges to the curriculum development because of the "ethics" subject matter. Moreover, in the delivery of that curriculum, in my opinion, a faculty member, in a university setting, should always lead discussions of subject matter in respectful, non-intrusive, non-confrontational ways, addressing "relevant" topics. This approach should allow faculty to avoid legal challenges regarding the "separation of church and state."

Chapter Eight – Anatomy of a Company

The Company

The places we work for are more than inanimate, faceless objects. Where we work are places of social interaction, places of friendships, places of frustration, and maybe places of toil. Companies are the personalities and experiences of the people who work there, who manage there, and who "live" there. Most Americans spend more time at their place of business and with their co-workers during their lifetimes than they do with their families. Social circle and friendships are most often made up of co-workers. Our culture has really integrated the workplace as the central hub of social interaction.

> *Companies are the personalities and experiences of the people who work there, who manage there, and who "live" there.*

Because of this importance in our lives, companies are really an extension of us. Just as we have a personality, feelings, beliefs, and attitudes, so in a sense do our companies. We give personal characteristics to companies when we describe them as healthy companies, compassionate companies, ruthless companies, and many others. Just as we have characteristics and health issues, so too, do our companies. Every company has an "anatomy" which directly reflects its health and its spirit.

The tribe

In our physical anatomy, the basic identification of who we are is the family that we were born to or tribe that we belong to. The same can be said for our spiritual anatomy as well. It is the tribe that roots us in our perceived reality. It is the tribe that both sustains us through its care, but also controls us in our behavior. Our leaders shape our basic beliefs, and we look to our "elders" as examples of what is expected and what behavior is appropriate.

We often believe that everyone in the business world is a type "A" mover and shaker; someone who is out to change the world and make their mark along the way. If this was true, then every company would be filled with only leaders and no followers; only managers and no workers. While it sometimes seems this way, the reality is that most of the employees in a company are the workers; they are the ones being lead and not leading. The "elders" are the managers and executives who are supposed to be exemplifying the morality of the tribe, the company. It is these individuals to whom the main responsibility for ethical behavior falls. They have to model what the company should be; not what they do, but what they should *be*.

> *The "elders" are the managers and executives who are supposed to be exemplifying the morality of the tribe, the company.*

Sometimes however, it is only the lone voice, or the prophet coming out of the desert that is saying what needs to be said. As I said in the Introduction, more often than not these prophets (regular employees) are not welcomed with open arms. They are seen as trouble makers. Their messages about ethics and morality are seen as naïve and unrealistic. They are dismissed as inexperienced; people who clearly don't understand the realities of business. The tribe does not like when one of its members breaks away to a new way of thinking. The tribe (the company) circles the wagons to protect itself and its own sense of reality.

The power

The next physical experience and next level of spiritual awakening in the individual is the sense of power and control that they have over their own destiny. For Maslow,[83] this was meeting the basic demands of shelter, food, survival – meeting the physiological and safety needs. As with the individual, the company too tries to develop its own sense of power and control. While this is a necessary part of company growth and experience, it is when executives can't move beyond (negative) power and control that the company suffers.

> *Often, the benevolent dictator isn't so benevolent, but just a dictator.*

Most of us have experienced a workplace that has been unable to grow beyond the need for coercive power and control. We see this in organizations which are lead by a "benevolent dictator"; usually those with an entrepreneurial founder and owner. Often, the benevolent dictator isn't so benevolent, but just a dictator. Companies which face serious financial survival issues often rapidly fall to a power and control personality. The ability to move one's self or one's company beyond the petty power plays (and need for control) is made real in accepting the service component of life. Companies must recognize the difference

---

[83] Abraham Maslow developed the theory of a "hierarchy of needs". According to Maslow, human beings are motivated by unsatisfied needs. Maslow believed that until certain "lower" needs were met, "higher" needs could not be satisfied or even pursued. http://www.ship.edu/~cgboeree/maslow.html

between needs and wants; between personal survival and collective survival. The ability not to descend to the lowest level when faced with crisis is based entirely upon the ethics by which professional life is led.

Power we viewed as the desire for self-determination and security doesn't need to imply force. As I referred to earlier, in the book, *Power vs. Force – The Hidden Determinants of Human Behavior*, Dr. David R. Hawkins writes that "power arises from meaning. It has to do with motive, and it has to do with principal."[84] He also says that force depends on the lowest basic behaviors, appealing to crass "influence" actions and that positive power derived from ethical behavior "energizes, gives forth, supplies, and supports."[85] Maybe these are really more than "hidden determinants", but they certainly apply to corporate behavior!

Corporate safety and security need not sacrifice the morality on which the company should be based. By setting aside the individual's interests and accepting a reality different than Adam Smith's invisible hand, companies are able to create a better performance for both the firm and the individual. This is, in essence, what Nobel Prize winner John Nash proposed in his "Nash Equilibrium" for strategic non-cooperative games.[86] Basically, Nash showed how the best outcome for "rivals" was achieved through mutual gain and cooperation. This became the accepted theory of economic behavior, as evidenced by the awarding of the Nobel Prize in 1994. Nash recognized that outcomes

---

[84]David R. Hawkins, M.D., Ph.D., *Power vs. Force – The Hidden Determinants of Human Behavior*, (Carlsbad, CA., Hay House Inc., 1995), pg. 132.

[85] Hawkins, *Power vs. Force*, pg. 132-134.

[86] John Milner, *John Nash and "A Beautiful Mind"*, Notices of the AMS, Volume 45 Number 10, pg. 1329, American Mathematical Society, November 1998 as found at: http://www.stat.psu.edu/news/conferences/JohnNash/milnor.pdf

couldn't be affected by changing only an individual's own st
it was necessary to change the strategy of all.[87] Corporate
security (like Maslow's "lower" needs) come from pursuing common
satisfaction not from individual domination.

The identity

When finding its own identity, companies face the same irrational
ideas of developing character and self-esteem as people do. How we
think *others* see us usually drives our own understanding of "who we
are". We look outward to figure out our sense of identity and self
esteem. Company identity is no different. Unfortunately, it shouldn't
be what others think of us that drives our sense of personal or corporate
identity, but our own understanding of self. This understanding (of self
worth) is based on whether we regularly reflect the values we hold
through the actions we take.

Corporate identity emerges from the continuing journey of its
people and all the challenge the journey entails. When we hear of the
"culture" of a company (its identity), we are really hearing about what
shaped the company from the struggles it has endured. These
experiences, and the behavior they reflect, drive what the identity has
become. Identity becomes the corporate culture. The best companies in
the world are renowned for their unique cultures, and those cultures are
usually embracing and inviting. These are the kinds of companies that
Fortune Magazine selects each year as it top "Top 100 Best Places to
Work".

---

[87] *Ibid.*, pg. 1330, "Nash introduced the fundamental concept of *equilibrium point*: a collection of
strategies by the various players such that no one player can improve his outcome by changing
only his own strategy."

Unfortunately, not all individuals and all companies have the ability, longevity, nor the personal strength to persevere through the development of identity. Companies begin to "believe their own press clippings", that is, believe what they say about themselves versus what is really happening. Instead of being inspirational and selfless, the leaders are autocratic and selfish. Instead of nurturing a corporate identity that is honorable, the company and its leaders accept a culture that is self-serving. Without a frame of reference from which to draw its accepted and expected behavior, a company is unable to create the identity that can serve it best. It is because of this that business cannot exist in a secular vacuum. Companies must draw on the religious and spiritual traditions that best exemplify the characteristics which enable us to achieve our highest potential.

The heart

A company that has heart.....what a marketing cliché that has become. It is unfortunate that this is the case. Being identified as having a heart can be a great virtue to a company. Heart has become cliché due to corporations like Wal-Mart, who are trying to bail themselves out of continuing ethical blunders towards their employees and suppliers.[88] Instead of truly being ethically-based and focusing on satisfying its customers through its product and services, these companies spend all their time on trying to convince the public how good they are. It sounds like Queen Gertrude saying in Shakespeare's Hamlet, "The lady doth protest too much, methinks."[89]

---

[88] Charles Fishman, *"The Wal-Mart You Don't Know"*, *Fast Company Magazine*, pg 68, December 2003.

[89] William Shakespeare, *Hamlet*, Act III, Scene II, (3.2.242), 1603.

> *Heart has become cliché due to corporations like Wal-Mart, who are trying to bail themselves out of continuing ethical blunders towards their employees and suppliers.*

Companies with heart are most often recognized by the ways in which they seek to enrich the lives of their employees. One company who displays tremendous heart is the software giant SAS Institute. Continually recognized as among the best companies in the world, SAS provides its employees a "work campus" to provide a balanced work and personal life. Its campus in Cary, NC, includes a high school and a middle school for its employees, on-site healthcare (doctors, clinics, and massage therapy), multiple health clubs and recreational services, and many other lifestyle amenities.

Heart is at the true nature of what a company can become. Heart is where passion for business turns into compassion for those affected by the business. Heart is how selfishness is transformed into selflessness. Heart is the part of the business that does not hide from its desire to be ethical. To be considered a company with heart may be the highest praise possible. Heart, however, needs to be governed also by wisdom, which I will talk about soon. Without wisdom, heart can be naïve and easily destroyed.

The voice - company choice

Whether in one's own life or in the life of a company, things don't just happen. The experiences of life and the directions taken are all determined by choice. Choice is most often seen as the conscious decisions that are made every day. However, choice can also be the lack of conscious decision – or at least the pretense of lack of consciousness. In either case, choice really is a matter of will. Will is the strength of character that is reflected in every decision made.

> *Will is the strength of character that is reflected in every decision made.*

Will in a company is exhibited by the daily choices made by the company directors, its executives and managers, and by its employees. Where a company allows individuals to engage in questionable activities, or operate with uncertain ethics, the company itself suffers. Its expression of self-identity is a reflection of the true nature of a company, not an exception to it. The "theory" of ethics becomes the "action" of moral behavior through company choice.

Corporate will, as expressed through its words and deeds, is more than an advertising trick or marketing gimmick. Ethical choice is not *convincing others* that the company <u>always</u> chooses the right path; it is simply always choosing the right path. The perceived value of a company isn't determined by what is said, but by what is done. Respect isn't earned by what is said, but by the integrity represented in corporate actions. Will is connecting the heart of a company with the mind of a company in a way that represents the best of what the company aspires to be.

The mind

The mind of the company is where all the logical decisions are made. By itself, the mind doesn't apply the concept of ethics in its decisions; it simply derives the "correct", logical choice. But the mind is also the place of creativity, ideas, and inspiration. The mind controls the rest of the functions of the company. It is in the company mind that the wisdom of ethical behavior is first understood. With this, the company mind must be accountable in setting the ethical direction that is to be taken.

Far too often, as has been highlighted throughout this book, the company mind seems to fail the rest of the corporate body in the decision that it makes, and in the lack of wisdom that it shows. The lack of wisdom does not necessarily occur in the nature of the decisions, but in an absence of understanding as to how those decisions become action. Here, the mind is not cooperating with the heart to lead to a correct choice. The absence of understanding is often rooted in the disconnect that the company mind (its directors and executives) has from the rest of the body, especially the employees, customers, and suppliers.

The spirit

Like the heart, the spirit of a company is an image that most of us understand. However, where the company with heart is sometimes seen as cliché; it is only through recognized performance that a company is considered to have spirit. Even beyond spirit, select companies who've demonstrated continuous, inspired leadership are described as having soul. Whether it's "company spirit" or "the soul of a company", these images portray the consciousness and the conscience of an organization.

> *There is no better way to describe the discovery of the soul of a company than the "achieving of harmony of the conscious and unconscious"*

Carl Jung spoke of the idea of the collective unconscious shaping our society. In a similar way, the company consciousness comes from the collective ethical consciousness of its employees. The website "The

Psi Café" describes the summary of Jung's work this way, "To Jung, the most important and lifelong task imposed upon any person is fulfillment through the process of individuation, achievement of harmony of conscious and unconscious, which makes a person one and whole."[90] There is no better way to describe the discovery of the soul of a company than the "achieving of harmony of the conscious and unconscious". When every aspect of the behavior of a company unites its actions (conscious) with its beliefs (unconscious), the essence of what a company can be becomes reality.

The 16th century Spanish Catholic mystic, St. John of the Cross, spoke of "the dark night of the soul" where we seem to be in a vast wasteland on our journey toward the divine.[91] To John, making it through the journey of the dark night is necessary as a person seeks a greater spiritual connectedness. The same is true for the spirit of a company. When growing from doing what is socially right to what is morally right, a company (and its owners, executives, and employees) goes through its own dark night where its commitment to moral action may simply seem like a waste of time. There doesn't appear to be any immediate benefits; there seems to be an endless series of falling back to uncertain behaviors; and there may even be a negative reaction from all the constituents.

True individual and corporate spiritual character is derived by making it through experiences that seem like a dark night. The sustainable nature of what a company can become happens when the

------

[90] http://www.psy.pdx.edu/PsiCafe/KeyTheorists/Jung.htm

[91] Saint John of the Cross, *Dark Night of the Soul*, Translated by E. Allison Peers, Image Books, New York, January 1959, uncopyrighted.

ethically and morally right choices are made in the times that are most difficult. It is in the company spirit that legendary companies are made.

Each January Fortune Magazine selects the "100 Best Companies to Work For." This annual list is always an interesting mix service companies, manufacturers, retailers, and more. Recent winners of this distinction have included NetApp in 2009, Google in 2007 & 2006, and Genetec in 2006. One of the most interesting was the 2005 winner Wegmans. Wegmans is an east coast grocer that was opened in 1930 by John and Walter Wegman. In an unlikely industry to be selected as the top company to work for, Wegmans truly is a company with a soul. In describing what makes Wegmans so unique, Darrell Rigby of the consulting firm Bain & Co. says that "You cannot separate their strategy as a retailer from their strategy as an employer."[92] In this, Fortune's selection of Wegmans acknowledges that the retailer has created a culture both inside and out where people matter, whether employee or customer; "the proof is in the stores every day. The smiles you receive from Wegmans employees are not the vacuous, rehearsed grins you get at big-box retailers. They are educated smiles, with vast stores of knowledge behind them...."[93] Wegmans recognizes the responsibilities that it has to both its employees and customers and by creating a culture of service and satisfaction, Wegmans has enabled service to flourish. Amount other things, Wegmans "lets no customer leave unhappy"; is, according to operations chief Jack DePeters, a $3 billion company run by 16 year old cashiers; foster creativity and development at all levels; and has created a company "culture" which is bigger than Danny

---

[92] Ellen Florian Kranz, *Fortune Magazine*, "*The 100 Best Companies to Work For*", January 24, 2005, pg. 66.

[93] *ibid*

Wegman.[94] By 2009 Wegmans had slowly fallen to number 5 in the Fortune ratings (#2 in '06, #3 in '07 and '08), showing that remaining the benchmark in performance is a difficult task.

Questions to Consider

1) In shaping the values of the company "tribe", do your members support or resist a move toward greater ethical accountability?

2) How does power play out in your company? Is it constructive or coercive?

3) Is your company identity based on the self assurance of doing the right thing; convincing others of what your identity is; or is it shaped by what you think others see or want to see?

4) Do the intentions of your company reflect compassion and selflessness, and earn the description of having heart? Or does the description of being heartless really fit?

5) When faced with choice, can your company claim to make the right choice every time? Does a "will" exist reflecting a consciousness of ethical and moral behavior.

6) Does wisdom prevail in the mind of your company? Are creation, inspiration, and insight married to logic when "thinking" about the decisions that affect the future of the company?

7) Is there an ethical company spirit in your workplace? Can you really "touch" the soul of your company?

---

[94] E. Kranze, *"The 100 Best"*, pg. 68.

Interview with Dr. Caroline Myss, PhD.

Dr. Caroline Myss is a New York Times bestselling author. In 1996, Caroline's book *Anatomy of the Spirit* was published, and became a New York Times best-seller. A year later, she wrote *Why People Don't Heal and How They Can*, which also became a best-seller, followed three years later by *Sacred Contracts*, her third consecutive New York Times best-seller. In 2004, she has added to the New York Times best-seller list with her latest book: *Invisible Acts of Power*.

A native of the Chicago area, Dr. Myss received a Masters Degree in theology from Mundelein College (Loyola), her PhD. from Greenwich University, and her B.A. in journalism from St. Mary of the Woods College in Indiana. Caroline Myss founded Stillpoint Publishing in 1981 with Meredith Young and Jim Young. Working with holistic doctors, Myss co-authored *The Creation of Health* with Dr. Norman Shealy, began creating audiotapes, and lecturing around the world.

Q)   Based on the work you have done in understanding the way in which the spiritual and physical health of individuals are interrelated, would you agree that a similar relationship exists in the health of a company and the and its "spiritual" characteristics?

A)   I absolutely agree that the paradigm of the body/mind/spirit applies to a "corporate body" as authentically as this paradigm applies to the individual. Within the corporate body, this paradigm represents or resonates to the fundamental law of the universe which is, "What is in one is in the whole"; that is, the consciousness of one person is reflected within the body of the whole corporation and the whole corporation is carried within the soul of the individual. This principle applied to simple biology can be easily validated - one cell tissue in the human body contains the DNA code for the entire body. There is no separation on the level of energy and a corporation is an energy network as well as a physical body of communication.

Q)   Business researchers have shown that 'ethical" companies are more profitable over the long-term than traditional companies. From your perspective, how would you explain this "health" especially where service to others is involved?

A)   Ethics are a factor of conscience far more than consciousness. A person participating in acts against his conscience does so in complete awareness of his actions. To do that, that individual must consciously violate his principles and his ethics, which requires that he repress the natural instincts of his soul. This action has significant consequences to the spirit of the corporate body - toxic, poisonous consequences that cannot be done away with simply by rationalizing one's behavior with a, "Well, it's just business" mantra. One's soul records acts of conscious violation. Eventually atmospheres are contaminated as these actions filter down through the ranks and employees lose respect for the elders of the corporation. Once respect is lost, the rest is history.

Q)   There is a saying in business "fake it until you make it". How long can you "fake" ethical behavior before it becomes part of who/what you are?

A)   That varies from person to person. Some people are capable of faking a lack of ethics for a lifetime, or until they are caught. I'm not sure how many people eventually see the light on their own. Certainly most people will continue in their unethical ways so long as there is a profit in it.

Q)   What would you recommend to business leaders in how to shape the ethical behavior of their employees, themselves, and their companies? Can they create a moral character of their companies?

A)   Nothing is more powerful than the personal example of a congruent individual at the helm...That's it and that's everything....

Epilogue

In the final analysis, for businesses and businesspeople to be successful, there must be a fundamental shift in thinking about business, in our behavior in business and in our view of what and who business is in business for. Our culture has moved beyond a willingness to accept things as they are and now is beginning to demand a higher level of performance and accountability at all levels.

International and global competition, communication, and trade have eliminated the corporate blinders that shielded workers, customers, suppliers, and communities from the possibility of what may be. No longer does the imbalance of power exist between the constituents. In the new equilibrium, a new paradigm is needed.

Situational, relative, or proportional ethics are simply insufficient to sustain business enterprises. The subtleties of each encounter require an unwavering foundation of belief and guiding principle. Without this, any organizational framework will collapse under the weight of its own uncertainty.

To succeed in this environment, businesses must assume a character that stems from, but transcends its leaders. Foundations of faith, when properly understood, provide for the unwavering foundation on which solid commercial organizations can be built.

When strong and durable organizational frameworks are built on solid and stable foundations, organizations will find themselves capable of *Defying the Trend*, and remain successful, profitable, and ethical.

Index